Missing

SHELLEY MACKENNEY

with John F. McDonald

PENGUIN BOOKS

PENGUIN BOOKS

Published by the Penguin Group
Penguin Books Ltd, 80 Strand, London WC2R ORL, England
Penguin Group (USA) Inc., 375 Hudson Street, New York, New York 10014, USA
Penguin Group (Canada), 90 Eglinton Avenue East, Suite 700, Toronto, Ontario, Canada M4P 2Y3
(a division of Pearson Penguin Canada Inc.)
Penguin Ireland, 25 St Stephen's Green, Dublin 2, Ireland (a division of Penguin Books Ltd)
Penguin Group (Australia), 707 Collins Street, Melbourne, Victoria 3008, Australia
(a division of Pearson Australia Group Pty Ltd)
Penguin Books India Pvt Ltd, 11 Community Centre, Panchsheel Park, New Delhi – 110 017, India
Penguin Group (NZ), 67 Apollo Drive, Rosedale, Auckland 0632, New Zealand
(a division of Pearson New Zealand Ltd)
Penguin Books (South Africa) (Pty) Ltd, Block D, Rosebank Office Park,
181 Jan Smuts Avenue, Parktown North, Gauteng 2193, South Africa

Penguin Books Ltd, Registered Offices: 80 Strand, London WC2R ORL, England

www.penguin.com

First published 2014
001

Copyright © Shelley Mackenney and John F. McDonald 2014
All rights reserved

The moral right of the author has been asserted

Set in 12.5/14.75pt Garamond MT Std
Typeset by Jouve (UK), Milton Keynes
Printed in Great Britain by Clays Ltd, St Ives plc

ISBN: 978–0–718–17938–0

www.greenpenguin.co.uk

MIX
Paper from
responsible sources
FSC® C018179

Penguin Books is committed to a sustainable
future for our business, our readers and our planet.
This book is made from Forest Stewardship
Council™ certified paper.

*To my wonderful daughter, Alyssia, who brought light
into my world when everything was dark.
By far the best thing that's ever happened to me.
I'm so thankful to be blessed with you.*

*To Nan, who always stood by me.
You will always be my best friend.*

To family and friends – if I hurt you at any time, I'm so sorry.

To everyone who helped me – I will never forget your kindness.

And to 'The Voice' – I love you always.

Contents

I

Leaving

It's all a haze – a mist that's come and settled in my mind. I'm moving in slow motion towards the coach station at Victoria. The sounds around me are dull and indistinguishable – voices and traffic noises, music playing somewhere in the distance, like a dream. My feet are moving, but not actually touching the pavement, they're on marshmallows or cushions or blown-up balloons. I'm not Shelley Mackenney any more. I'm someone else, born again, like a child.

I woke up early that morning. I felt hyperactive and my legs were shaking in the bed, despite the antidepressants, and I knew what I had to do. Something in my head told me. I felt nothing – no hurt, no guilt, no relief, no fear. Nothing. I didn't know how I was going to do it, just that I had to.

I've already dismantled my mobile phone and thrown it away. Don't misunderstand me, I love my family despite all their faults – but the normal rules of life no longer apply. Nothing else matters now.

The ticket window appears before me and the ghost of a woman looks out. Her mouth is moving but, for a while, no words come through her greyish teeth. I try to focus on her face and eventually her voice reaches me from inside the ticket-office window.

'Where to?'

'What?'

'Where are you going?'

'I don't know.'

She gives me a look, one of those looks that insinuates I'm either an idiot or a practical joker and she's in no mood for either.

I'm aware of people queuing behind me. I can hear their sighs and snarls and the smell of their impatience. I don't look round.

'You'll have to step aside if . . .'

'The first coach.'

'What?'

'The first coach out of here.'

Then her voice slips back inside her mouth and she swallows it and I can't hear it any more. I give her some money and she gives me a ticket and points to the left. I find a coach with the engine already running and I get on it – climb slowly up the steps and hand the ticket to the leering driver and make my way down the aisle to the back.

Other people are already on board. They have no faces that I can see and they look at me through black recesses where their eyes should be as I pass them. The coach is a mile long and it takes me an hour to get to my seat. There's a thumping sound somewhere, a foetal heartbeat under the floor, and I know there must be some kind of demon down there. Or maybe it's just the noise of the engine. But I keep my feet up close to me just in case, until the coach begins to pull out of the station – and the rhythm of its movement lulls me into a false sense of security and my eyes close.

It was warm that morning when I first woke – 27 May 2002. It was bright enough for me to see round the bedroom, even though I'd tried my best to block out the light. Thin blades of sun cut through the slots in the blinds I hadn't opened in days. But now it was Monday and I had to face the world again, face the stuff I hated – people and money and responsibility and family and littleness and life. I felt I was being ground down by the routine of everything, churned up in its cogwheels. I would have to get up and put on my happy face again – my smile and my style and my guile. I felt so tired. More than tired – fatigued. Maybe it was the Prozac; the dosage was becoming stronger by the day because the doctor thought he was wiser than he really was. The antidepressants weren't all bad, though. They made me walk around in a daze, but they stopped me eating and I'd lost fifty pounds in weight. Everybody was saying how fit I looked – how fabulous!

I reached for my cigarettes. I was smoking sixty a day; maybe I was trying to slowly poison myself. I could hear the music of Capital Gold floating up from downstairs, lingering on the smoke swirls. Then Nan shouted up.

'Shell . . . I got you a tea here!'

I'd lived with Nan since I was three, since my mother walked out in the middle of the night and left me on my own in the house full of silent resentment. Nan came and found me crying. She broke the door open and rescued me and had been there for me ever since.

To really understand my grandmother, you'd have to read her book *Borstal Girl*, and you'd know she was the toughest woman in the world back then. Nobody messed with Eileen Mackenney and those who did – police or villains or solicitors or smartarses – soon got a bashing, in one way or another.

My family were, and still are, the Mackenneys. Granddad 'Big H' was serving life in prison for five murders he didn't commit; Dad 'Harry Jnr' was on the run; and then there were my uncles John and Daniel, who were tough men too. I have no memories of my mother before she left and the memory of her leaving is all in a kind of third-person perspective – as if I'm outside myself, just observing. But, even though I didn't realize it at the time, it had a devastating effect on my life. It was a trauma that haunts me to this very day.

She was angry the night she left. Edgy. Unapproachable. Her nerves were pared and naked. She put me in a back room and I remember looking down at a green and brown blanket that spread itself across the floor. I remember feeling confused, then frightened, when I couldn't get out of the room. The house was eerily silent and I felt completely alone. Everything was dark and I was crying. I don't know how long it was before Nan started banging on the door. I could hear her shouting.

'Shelley! Shelley!'

I called back in my little voice.

'Nan! Nan!'

It comes back to me in sudden flashbacks, that night – like replaying different parts of an old film. Then the door got smashed in and Nan was picking me up and wrapping her coat round me and carrying me away.

I stayed with her at 49 Crutchley Road in southeast London until I was twenty-two.

My mother left me with many issues. I've always felt unwanted and unloved and lonely, even though I've been surrounded by people since then. I wondered if it was something I did that made her leave me like that. Why did she leave me? Other mothers loved their children. What was wrong with me that my mother didn't?

Couldn't?

Nan tried so hard to substitute for her. She loved me with all her heart and soul, but she was fighting her own battles with police and courts and villains and violence. She always tried to be there for me and I owe her the whole world, but I didn't feel I belonged anywhere and that feeling lingered all through my growing up. My mother didn't want me, and if *she* didn't, how could anyone else? I felt like a burden, guilty for being born.

When Nan took me in, I went into a world of adults: Eileen and my elusive father and my big uncles. It was a man's world, full of brutal violence and raids on the house and police stations and courthouses and prisons. I felt isolated, even though they were very protective of me and would never allow anything to happen to me. I felt different and that difference followed me around like a shadow.

My family are fighters, fierce people with fierce personalities. They're fearless and free willed; they rush in without worrying about consequences. I was passive, reserved – shrinking, even. I felt I had nothing in common with them. I didn't understand them and they didn't understand me. My father was on the run when my mother left and I didn't really know him. He was someone I saw every so often for a fleeting moment and then he was gone, vanishing into the distant sound of sirens and quickening heartbeats. Nan took me everywhere with her, even at a very young age – to fights and riots and punch-ups and dust-ups and midnight dashes to hospitals and filthy cells.

I was always there.

I remember a big fight in the Joiner's Arms pub when Uncle John was seriously stabbed and his friend was murdered and Nan was fighting with police, desperate to find out what had happened to her sons. On another occasion, I remember our house being attacked by a mob and watching down the hall towards the front door as they tried to smash their way in with iron bars. I've gone round the pubs and clubs with Nan at night searching for my dad and uncles to warn them there was trouble heading their way. Everyone would look at us when we walked in – Eileen Mackenney and her little gaping granddaughter. But Nan was afraid of nothing and she'd keep searching, even in the men's toilets, until she found her boys.

I saw all this from the time Nan took me into her house – the violence and the intimidation – and I didn't like it, didn't understand why we had to put up with it all.

If you want to know what it was really like, then you have to read *Borstal Girl*, which is Nan talking and telling it her own way.

But, from my point of view, it was harrowing. Cruel. Cold-blooded. I knew it wasn't the life I wanted for when I grew up and became a person. My family seemed to get stronger with every bloody brawl and every police perversion and every judicial miscarriage, but I began to hate it. I didn't want this life, I wanted things to be different. I wanted to be someone else, to travel a quieter, saner path. I wanted to do well in school and get a good job and maybe get married and buy a house – you know, the kind of normal things that normal people do. I wanted to take care of my nan when she got old, take her away from the violence and the bloodshed and the tragedy of it all, show her there was more to life than always being on the brutal side of the bars – on the lying side of the law. I wanted to give her a good way of life, where she didn't have to worry or fight or run across London thinking her sons had been shot or stabbed.

With everything that was happening around us, the family were paranoid about my safety. They didn't trust anybody from the outside and things became extremely tight on the inside. Everyone knew what was going on with everyone else. Cousins, uncles, nephews, they all came to see Nan, and if one had a problem, all the others would be there to sort it out. Maybe it sounds like the way a family should be, and I'm sure it was in some respects. But there was no privacy, nowhere to hide from the heaviness of it all. The family came first and there was no room for the individual. With all these strong personalities in such claustrophobic proximity, tempers flared regularly. My family didn't have verbal rows, they had full-blown battles. But if someone from the outside tried to intervene or take them on, they'd all come together in a self-defensive stance. I wasn't allowed to go anywhere on my own – and I mean anywhere! I always had a 'minder' with me. If other kids said anything to me, Nan would be straight up the school attacking their parents. Because my grandfather was in prison for murder, some of my classmates whispered that he'd killed my mother, but after being attacked a few times, they said nothing at all.

Soon, the other kids were too scared to have anything to do with me and I didn't get invited to birthday parties or after-school clubs or sleepovers or into team sports. But it didn't bother me. Strange, really: I grew up on a very rough estate, my family were outlaws, I knew more about the location of local police stations than parks, my mother was gone and my father was on the run – anyone would've thought I'd just go feral. But I didn't, I went the opposite way. I loved school. I loved learning and I absorbed everything like a thirsty man at an oasis. I was the first person in my family to have a real education and that set me further apart. It hung on me like a scent. I didn't need to be pushed to do the work, it just found a natural home inside my head. I never missed a day of it, and the more I learned, the happier I was. The other kids left me alone and that suited me just fine. I didn't like people around me, fidgeting and flustering and making my flesh creep. I felt strongest when I was on my own, because people see your weaknesses when you let them in. When they get to know you.

I was sent to Catford County Girls' Secondary School when I was eleven. Nan would walk me there every day and she'd be waiting to walk me home when I came out. I told her I didn't need her to do it, it was a bit embarrassing at my age, but she said the streets were dangerous and she was just making sure I was left alone. I was beginning to feel a bit boxed in, smothered by all the minding and the arrests and fights and convictions and acquittals. I started doing a paper round when I was thirteen; Nan would come with me. And so it went on. I got after-school jobs in a pet shop and a garden centre, and a summer job in a baker's, and a Christmas temp job at Argos. Every time, Nan would come with me to work and be waiting for me outside when I finished, no matter what time of the night or day it was. I had to work to supplement the family income, because my father and uncles were often locked up in prison; and in the evenings I acted as the family secretary and solicitor, filling in forms and applications and affidavits, and reading witness statements and statutory rights reviews and evidence and the rules of policy and practice.

When other girls my age were going out at weekends and having boyfriends and learning how to interact, I was doing schoolwork or dealing with family issues or running round police stations and courthouses and hospitals in the middle of the night. Because I was always surrounded by adults, I felt older than my years. I was never carefree, like a teenager should be. I worried a lot, always stressed out about the hand-wringing poverty, or if Dad was going to be caught, or if the house would be raided again. I missed that part of growing up where I was supposed to experiment with boys and alcohol and all the other girly teenager things, like attitude and affectation and awkwardness.

My father was finally apprehended, after being on the run for many years, and sent to prison. I was seventeen when he came out again and I was becoming a woman. Inside, time had stood still for Dad and he expected me to be the girl I was when he went away. He saw that boys were paying attention to me and that made him more protective than ever. To him I was still his little girl and he didn't know how to adjust to the changes that had happened to me while he'd been in prison.

So, the claustrophobic protection got worse. I was pretty and men looked at me and tried to talk to me – those who didn't know the family, a family that considered everyone outside it to have an ulterior motive for everything. I remember once when I was in a kebab shop and Nan was outside chatting, some man wouldn't let me pass – the only way for me to get out was to squeeze tightly against him. I made the mistake of telling Nan later, who told one of my uncles, who caught the man next day and threw him in the back of a van, gave him a beating and dumped him miles away from Catford. That was the way my family operated. The people they associated with were ruthless, whichever side of the law they were on, and they were afraid I'd get hurt – one way or another. The eye they kept on me grew sharper and more suspicious of anybody I came into contact with. And I knew it would all end in tragedy and tears, but I didn't know how or when.

When I started work at Argos, I was told I had to open a bank account. I got chatting to the lady who interviewed me for the account and, because my grades at school were so good, the bank offered me a full-time job. I was hoping to do A-level chemistry and physics and maths – I was interested in genetic engineering and I wanted to go to university. However, after years of hardship and persecution, we didn't have much money and life was a constant struggle. I didn't have many clothes, my bed was broken and I was sleeping on a mattress on the floor. Every day was a huge effort for Nan to make ends meet, to hold everything together. I hated seeing her having to struggle all the time. The bills kept coming in and she'd always make do, always sort things in her own stoical way. So, when I was offered a full-time job in the bank, I took it. It gave me the chance to bring some decent money into the house and make things easier for her. As well as that, it was a way to get away from my life as a non-person, drifting on a sea of complacency. But, of course, I had to give up on the A-levels – something I've always regretted.

I was seventeen when I started work at the bank, in November 1997. I was a very clean-living girl. I'd never drunk alcohol or done drugs. I'd been to an all-girls school and had never been clubbing or out with boys. I was naive about sex and all the other stuff I should have been learning about as part of teenage life, instead of the constant confidence trick of crime and punishment.

I was a cashier to begin with – money in and money out, and other routine counter work. I was also sent on lots of customer-focus courses and I was trained in all the different types of financial products the bank offered to the unsuspecting borrower. I let it all in and I loved it. It was a new life and it was getting me out of the house, away from the old life – even though either Nan or Dad, when he came out of prison, still took me to work every day and met me for lunch and picked me up in the evenings. They even went with me to do the courses I was sent on. Despite all that, I found I had a natural flair for the work, especially the selling. I also found it ironic, to be working in a bank and coming from a family of alleged bank robbers.

And I smiled inside.

But I was no crook. I was a straight-and-narrow woman. There would be no looking over my shoulder from now on. Before, everyone I came into contact with knew me as the 'Mackenney girl' and that was enough for them to form an opinion of me without even knowing me. Here at the bank, they didn't know about my family history and I could reinvent myself. I was judged only on my performance in my job – and I was good at that. I was now rubbing shoulders with intelligent, professional women who wore the latest designer clothes and drove smart cars and owned their own houses. I admired them. I wanted to be like them – thought I could at last learn about the attitude and affectation, though maybe not the awkwardness.

I became addicted to work. I loved the atmosphere of sureness and sophistication that enveloped me like a new skin. I volunteered for overtime and extra days, so I could stay with my new life and away from my old one. It was fun, it was full-on and it was fabulous. I quickly went from cashier to receptionist, dealing with queries and complaints, then new accounts and direct referrals, while gaining supervisory experience helping new staff and maintaining the smooth-running of the branch. I was impressed by the important sound of these responsibilities, by their sureness and smart facades. I started interviewing customers – basic stuff to start with, like processing credit card and loan applications. But soon I was selling mortgages and insurance products and advising on long-term investments until, finally, I was promoted to branch advisor.

I had my own diary and desk and a book of sales appointments, and I felt that I belonged here, with the rest of the sagacious women with the power suits and sophisticated smiles. Here, at least, I was treated like I was someone of worth, not just a silly girl who didn't know what was good for her. I found a sense of freedom I'd never known before. I could sometimes stagger my lunch break and get to walk around on my own, without anyone shuffling along beside or behind me to keep an intolerant eye on me. The clients listened to me with interest. I could show them what I was really made of and I knew they weren't just humouring me like they were at home. My family thought they knew everything and I was young and stupid and needed protecting because I wasn't able to do it for myself. At work, I felt I had independence and free-dom and respect. I could grow.

My spiral into debt began slowly. At first I was too young to borrow money, but once I turned eighteen, all the credit doors swung open and the light of floating debt flooded through. I couldn't believe it – the world suddenly turned to gold. These were the heady days before credit crunches, fiscal contraction and recession, and banks were still throwing money at people – people on the dole and in mental hospitals and people who were dead and even people who weren't the people they said they were. Anybody could get credit. My bank account was upgraded and I was given an overdraft and a cheque book and a debit card and a credit card, along with my monthly salary. I didn't understand the implications of debt, how it could spread like blood spilling from an artery, or how very, very ugly it could get – how it could turn the gold to guilt in your hands.

The first thing I did was buy a new bed and a new carpet for my bedroom – then Nan and I went shopping! Suddenly there were many, many ways to buy the things I wanted. Buy now, bleed later. In any case, overdrafts didn't need to be paid back and a minimum monthly payment on the credit cards was enough to ensure I was offered bigger and better ones. As my artificial income started to increase, so did my very real expenditure. I could have anything I wanted, and so could my family. It wasn't long before I established myself as the main breadwinner in the house. It was easy at first, floating on the bubble, buying little things here and there. It was good to give. Then it became an obligation, expected. Not immediately – but gradually. Over time.

'Shelley will take care of that.'

But in wanting to fix everything for everyone, I was breaking myself.

Now all I see through my closed eyelids on the coach to nowhere are the slicing blades of sunlight through the Monday-morning blinds, and Nan with my tea ready downstairs and me having to get up and face the world again. Nobody knows about the dreams I'm having, the nightmares – where I'm dying and I never wake up, and I'm happy because I don't *want* to wake up. They don't know I can't eat, or about the debt, or that I need to pay the mortgage arrears by tomorrow. If I don't, the bank will start repossession proceedings. Nan's lived in this house for thirty-five years and I can't let that happen! And Dad's rent needs to be sorted – he showed me his notice to quit yesterday. And the council tax got mixed up and now I have to pay three years' arrears.

I brush my teeth and wash my face and dress slowly, languidly, in T-shirt and jeans and baseball cap and hoodie. I don't work for the bank any more – now I work in a betting shop, full of yellow fingernails and rasping voices and leering looks and desperation. It's just a means to an end, till I get something better. Downstairs, Nan is stressing over something or other, which is her way, and Dad and my uncles are eating breakfast. Nan has tea and toast waiting for me.

'Why are you wearing that 'orrible hat, Shell? It looks awful.'

I ignore her and go to the fridge. I have to know if we need food. The post drops through the letter box – bills and reminders and threats and last-chance letters with big red final demands scrawled across them, their shrillness shrieking at me from behind the brown envelopes. Gas bills and water rates and council tax and loan payments and credit cards and mortgage demands – all overdue! Dread fills me and my stomach churns. I wish someone could help me, but there is no one – only me. I've been taking care of everything for so long, it doesn't occur to anyone that I might need some help myself.

I need more than help – I need a miracle.

My hands shake so I can't drink the tea and my heart feels like it's going to beat right out of my chest. I have to ride this panic attack, to calm myself. I light another cigarette and pop a Prozac. It works. I drink the tea and I stash the bills in my bag. I smile. I'm a pretender – practised and professional. I have to get to work because I need the money. It's not nearly what I was earning at the bank, but it's only till I get something better. I wait at the front door while Nan gets her coat because she still goes everywhere with me, takes me everywhere. I'm running out of cigarettes and we go round the long way to the betting shop so I can get some. At the newsagent's, I buy an ice lolly – I don't know why, I'm not thinking straight. Nan looks at me like I'm mad, eating an ice lolly at eight in the morning.

It takes me twenty minutes to walk up the hill to work and I remember talking to Nan but I don't remember what about. My mind is in overdrive, trying to figure out how I'm going to fix everything. We arrive at the betting shop and I say goodbye to Nan. It never crosses my mind that I won't be seeing her again – for a very long time.

2
Trauma

The coach is travelling fast and I like the speed. It's taking me further and further away, like some benign abductor. My eyes open every now and then, and I see other vehicles passing to and fro like phantoms on the motorway. I can't remember where I'm going, but it doesn't matter. The Prozac is numbing my brain and it's like I've turned a switch off. All the things that worried me, filled me with dark dread, are gone now. I have no more responsibility – I have nothing to fix, nothing to put right. The pounding heartbeat on the underbelly of the coach is silent now and I know the demon is no longer down there. I allow my feet to fall to the floor – and the round rhythm of the wheels takes me back to a time when I was in another vehicle and I was drifting on the day – just like now. It was my father's old Rover and we were singing together as we cruised along. I loved to sing back then, even in my isolation; singing was something that made my heart soar and stopped the memories I didn't have of my mother.

When I was younger, my father taught me everything he would have taught a son. I learned about cars – how to repair them and what tools were needed to do the job. I learned about criminality and the law and that there was no real difference between the two. There was a complete gym in Nan's house and I'm not talking about those little plastic things that girls lift – no, it was all big men's stuff. I'd be out working with Dad on the cars, seeing engines being souped up and fetching the tools for him. I learned all about electrical alarms and locks and how to patch into police radio signals. The walls of the house were covered with samurai swords and crossbows and maces and nunchucks – not exactly girly lavender and lace. And all the men of the family would come round and Nan would hold court and it was like that 80s' television programme *Bread* – only a lot more serious and table-thumping.

I was close to my father, despite not knowing him very well. I knew him in the sense of him being a hard man, someone the police had it in for, and someone who taught me things about cars and how to protect myself in a fight and stuff like that. But I don't think I knew him emotionally – the real man, the man inside. The men in my family didn't allow their emotions to show. It was dangerous to do that. But every now and then he'd let his guard slip and we'd sing. We'd go driving in his Rover car and if he saw the police, he'd speed up and they'd chase us and it was frightening and fun – a game that wasn't a game. I loved the speed and, even now, I drive too fast. Once, when I was about fourteen and we were on a dual carriageway, doing about forty mph – it was winter and late in the afternoon, getting dark and dusky – I was in the passenger seat and Dad suddenly spotted a police car tailing us. My father could spot an unmarked cop car a mile away. That was it, we were off. He was weaving in and out of the lanes, doing seventy, and there was a traffic jam building up in front of us. The police had their flashing lights and sirens on now and other police cars had joined in the chase as the traffic moved to let them through.

Dad jumped the lanes and was speeding up the opposite side of the carriageway into oncoming traffic – how we didn't get smashed to smithereens was a miracle and my heart was trying to jump out of my mouth and make its own escape. We swerved from one lane to another, in between the oncoming cars. There was a cross junction at the top and the lights were red and, when we reached it, Dad did a full ninety-degree turn, crossing all the cars that were coming from the left, then a sharp right straight on to another dual carriageway. We took off so fast I thought we were going to *actually* take off and it bought my father some time, because the police couldn't get through the horn-beeping traffic that had stopped at all kinds of angles on the junction. We drove into some estate with rows and rows of flats like tall rectangular trees and made our way through the maze. Dad did a reverse manoeuvre into a space underneath a kind of overhang. He switched the engine off and we ducked down and listened to the sirens singing all around us – until they got tired of looking and went away.

A year later, I was in the car with him again. But this time he didn't escape. The police surrounded him – they came in plain clothes and boxed him in. We weren't far from Nan's house and Dad didn't try to fight, he just gave up. But they still beat him. For no reason other than spite. I'd seen Dad fight with police before and I was surprised he didn't this time. Maybe it was because I was with him and he didn't want me to get hurt. Or maybe he was tired of fighting – running – and just wanted it all to end.

Memories like that can come and sit inside my psyche sometimes and I get a feeling of wet-green warmth, like on a late-summer evening when you're sad about something but you don't know what it is. Some old nostalgia. Some fading fragrance of love. My family loved me in the way they knew how, in the way they learned to love. But when they put my father back in prison and my mother was long, long gone, I felt more than ever that there was something missing inside me. So I turned it round. Instead of feeling the pain of loneliness, I started to love being alone. I began building a wall against the outside world, where I was safe inside and no one could get to me to hurt me. I suppose it was a personal psychological extension of the physical protectiveness of my family. And I was never bored with my own company – I would paint and sculpt and knit and sew and sing. I sang all the time and the songs took me away to a different place and made me a different person. I sang until the crippling responsibility of debt and stomach-churning fret took all the songs away – and there was no music any more.

Before that happened, my life came back for a while and I was on top of my small personal world. I was in my element when I was at the bank – me and my business suit and six-inch heels – and I could sell things to people, things that wouldn't hurt them later on. I was honest with them and they liked me for that; they respected my integrity. And it felt good. I had my own office, where I'd interview and assess customers and I felt I was someone special, not just the 'Mackenney girl' any more. And it was easy, even with the overdrafts and credit cards and spiralling debt – at first. The minimum monthly payments were small to begin with, £30, £40, £50, and the offers of six-month interest-free balance transfers came in with smiling faces and outstretched helping hands. The more I spent my overdraft, the higher it was raised, and the credit limits on the cards kept going up all the time too. Then I discovered catalogues, because I was getting mountains of junk mail through the door all the time. I didn't realize – even though I should have – that a good credit rating gets passed round retail institutions like a plate at a church service. The catalogues were a great new way to get nice stuff for Nan's house and I ordered and ordered and ordered. I was on my way to a shopping addiction – or oniomania as they call it now – and it's a genuine addiction, just like people have to drugs or alcohol or gambling or greed.

Nan really loved her house at 49 Crutchley Road and she wanted to buy it. I was in the perfect place to provide a mortgage – or so I thought. But the bank refused my application. I was too far in debt and they knew it. When they offset my outgoings against my income, I wasn't even close to the amount I needed to borrow. That was the start of the slide, the Sisyphus summit of the charade, the moment when things inevitably started to go downhill. I went to a broker and lied about my financial situation and got a self-certified high-interest mortgage instead.

For a while, I wasn't aware that things had changed, that the upward trend had inverted itself to a downward spiral. I still took Nan shopping and bought takeaways for the whole family and spent hundreds of pounds on groceries – I always wanted to see the cupboards full of food because they never were when I was younger. I wanted my family to have everything: my family, who'd known nothing but hardship and persecution and prosecution, who'd had nothing before. Now they could have everything, and I'd pay for it. I was trying to prove that I could be useful, trying to prove my worth. Because, deep down, I believed I was worthless.

It started to get crazy. I remember walking past a furniture store with Nan that was selling an Italian-made dining table with six silk-upholstered chairs. Nan stopped to look at it and, when I got back to work, I ordered it and had it delivered the next day. The price was ridiculous, but I knew she liked it and that was enough. I had large bouquets of lilies made up and sent to her every week. I bought cookers and fridges and music systems with surround sound, and not just one, but two at a time. It was bizarre: here I was, advising bank customers how to consolidate debt and make repayments more affordable and reduce commitment and manage their money, yet I couldn't control my own spending. I even bought Nan an Aga cooker she didn't need, but by now she was getting worried about where all the money was coming from, so she rang up the shop and made them take it back.

That's when depression set in. By now I was using money from one credit card to pay off another. I still wasn't allowed to go out on my own, so I wasn't spending on myself. But the shopping became its own escape, a freedom of sorts. I could fade into the futility – sink into the surreality. Eventually, all the credit cards maxed out and the overdraft stopped growing and I had to seek out more dubious sources of credit – sources with interest rates that were dangerous. Destructive. Life-threatening. I started having really bad nightmares and panic attacks –

one was so bad I was rushed from work to hospital by ambulance because of the terrible chest pains and difficulty breathing. That's when they put me on Prozac and I went all funny in the head. All sort of furry and fuzzy. Flapping about like a flag in the wind. I became paranoid, thinking people were talking about me and that the house was cursed and there was something evil in the walls trying to get me to do bad things.

I contemplated setting fire to 49 Crutchley Road, with me in it; then all my problems would be solved. The only thing that stopped me was the thought of Nan on the streets in a cardboard box, a bagwoman. I dreamed I was walking round the house and there was blood everywhere, up all the walls, and dead people hanging from the ceiling, screaming at me. Then the dreams changed to dying – me drowning and falling off buildings and getting run over. And I was happy, happy to be ending this horrible life, relieved that I wouldn't wake up in the morning and have to face another day of fiscal misery.

I knew I was losing my mind when I started wanting to hurt people. I'd get into mad rages and boil with anger, then storm out of work because I couldn't trust myself not to strangle somebody. And I had no one to tell all these terrible torments to.

I can't remember a time when I didn't feel alone. Not 'on my own' alone, because from the time I went to live with Nan she was always with me, or someone else was. But I was emotionally alone. It was deep-rooted. I can't remember ever being part of something, apart from the bank. But, within the family, I felt no one wanted to be near me – I was an outsider looking in, an outcast, a spare part that had fallen off someone and wouldn't fit on any-one else. I felt like I was born to be alone and destined to journey through life like a castaway on a raft of coconut shells.

But the worst was yet to come. My new life with the bank, that had given me so much hope, was about to go up in flames of shame. The hundreds of pounds I'd bor-rowed from dubious sources to continue paying off debts and provide a decent life for my family had grown into thousands and it was becoming impossible to manage. It was a crazy thing to do in the first place, but unless you've been in my position, you'll never understand. It was a matter of getting from one month to the next – if I could just get through this month, then I could breathe for a while longer and maybe something would turn up before next month came round. Every payday, my entire salary was going to pay off the escalating interest rates. They would wait for me outside the bank and I'd have to hand over everything. It got worse and worse and worse, and I could see no way out.

It was affecting my work. I was walking into rooms and forgetting why I was there. I started to lose track of con-versations when I was talking to people. I couldn't remember what I was saying or what they were saying to me. I was forgetting everything and developed what's called dissociative amnesia. In times of heightened stress and unhappiness, the brain has a way of protecting itself by forgetting its problems. But it forgets everything else as well. I was forgetting about people's mortgages and the names of the products I was trying to sell. I was behind with my repayments to the loan sharks and they called me at work and told me if I didn't pay them money that day, they'd hurt someone. I had no money at all and nowhere to turn to for any. I could have told my family – my father and uncles – but this would have started a war and everybody would have suffered. My father was just out of prison and I didn't want him going straight back in again – and my uncles had their own problems to deal with. I was panic-stricken. Something in my head snapped and I went to the tills and took £1,000. I knew that was it, I was finished. I'd crossed the line and become what I never wanted to be – a thief! I felt sick to my stomach, because I knew I'd lost the one thing that was holding me together, helping me to maintain some semblance of sanity: my pride. My only reason to live was ripped away in a single moment.

And I gave up that day.

That night, I took an overdose of Nurofen and sleeping tablets in the hope that I could kill myself. End it all. It didn't work, just hyped me up, and I hardly slept. First thing next morning I rang my manager and told her what I'd done. I could have covered it up, I suppose, put it down as an error, switched things round, forged a document or two. But I knew if I started down that road I wouldn't be able to turn back – and what would that have made me? I was crying on the phone – babbling – mumbling – missing my words. I told her everything. It hurt so much, it tore me to pieces. Everything I'd ever wanted and worked for was gone.

And I wished I was gone too.

The bank was very civilized about it. I was suspended on full pay pending an enquiry. They could have had me arrested and maybe it would have been better if they had, if I'd been sent to prison like the rest of my family. A month later I was dismissed for gross misconduct. I was heartbroken. Devastated. Dead inside.

After I recovered from the breakdown and the failed suicide attempt, I had to sign on for social security. All my debts were on temporary hold as there was no way I could pay them. I felt totally degraded that first day applying for benefit – I felt everybody knew me, knew what I'd done, why I was there. My Jobcentre supervisor was a bank customer I used to advise and I could see the smirk underneath his false concern and officious form-filling. After prying into every aspect of my life, he eventually awarded me £50 a week to live on.

Although most of my debts were on hold, the sharks weren't. So I had to sell off everything I'd bought over the past four years, at a heavy backdoor discount. I also started making counterfeit CDs for the family as a way of earning extra money. I didn't really want to get involved in 'family business', but I was desperate for cash to keep the wolves at bay. This hand-to-loan-shark existence went on for about three months, then I got the job in the betting shop. I hated the place, full of false anticipation and utter dejection and the smell of premature old age.

I was only there for three weeks.

Now I leave Nan on the street and she says she'll see me at lunchtime – as usual. She doesn't know how I feel and I don't want her to. She has her own troubles. I go to my job, working out the odds and stamping the betting slips and deciphering the stakes. It's soul-destroying, sitting behind the glass partition for protection and watching all the fading dreams and disappointment. In a way, the ambience suits my own situation – I'm a no-hoper, just like all the others in this dreary place. Now that I have a job, my debts are no longer on hold and everyone is lining up for their money. There's nothing left to sell and I can't hold the bailiffs off much longer. It's like I'm in an invisible prison and, although I thought I saw a way out when I woke this morning, I can't remember what it was now.

Bloody Prozac!

Everything is closing in on me and there's no way out of the trap. A thousand nagging voices are screeching at me in my head.

'Pay this!'

'No, pay this!'

'You'll lose the house!'

'It's all your own fault!'

'You're useless!'

'Always will be!'

'Better if you were never born!'

I'm like an animal that's cornered and I suddenly get this urge to run – to get away – to escape somehow. The feeling gets stronger as I go through the morning. Lunchtime is normally 12.30 and Nan will be meeting me, but now they've asked if I can go early, at 11.30 instead. I leave the betting shop and find myself on my own. There's no one to keep a close eye on me. I can do it. I can do it now!

As soon as I decide to run, all the voices in my head stop. I don't know where to go. I have £40 in my pocket and I think about Catford train station, but someone might see me on the way. I can't stand here on the street, so I hail a black cab and tell him I have £10 and ask him to take me as far as he can for that.

'Which direction, miss?'

'I don't know, which direction are we facing?'

'North.'

'North, then.'

As the taxi moves away, I take out my mobile phone and turn it off. I know my family will be calling as soon as they realize I'm missing. I won't be able to cope with Nan's crying and begging me to come home, I'll melt inside and won't have the strength to go on. I dismantle the phone and throw it through the window and I can see the broken pieces in the road as I move further and further away. They're calling me to come back – pleading with me. I turn my eyes away and cover my ears with my hands, until they're too far away for me to hear.

The cab driver drops me at Clapham and I walk northwards towards the Thames. I think about throwing myself into the murky water but, instead, I cross over Vauxhall Bridge in a dream and keep moving until I see Victoria Coach Station up ahead. I still have £30 in my pocket and I drift in there. There's a queue at the ticket window and the paranoia comes back. I think that my family know exactly where I am – they have eyes all over the city. Any minute now I'll feel a hand on my shoulder. I pull my hood up over the baseball cap, as if it can hide me, disguise me, make me vanish. I'm not thinking about where I'm going to go or how I'm going to live – none of that is important right now. What's important is to get away.

I buy a ticket.
I board the coach.
The engine starts.
I'm twenty-two and, for the first time in my life –
I'm free!

3
New Life

When I descended from the coach in Birmingham, I was suffering from post-traumatic stress disorder – but I didn't know it at the time. In fact, I don't really know when the actual trauma occurred, except that it was in London, sometime before I left. I don't know if there was an actual specific moment, to be honest. It was a lot of little traumas that crept up on me and finally added up to one big trauma. The pressure just got worse and worse, and then the physical symptoms manifested themselves – the dreams and the shaking and the nervousness. I suppose the final disorientation probably came on the day I had to leave the bank for the last time and my dream of a different life disappeared. After that, things were never the same again.

I didn't feel any emotional stress that first evening in Birmingham. I felt free. I wasn't that old Shelley Mackenney any more, the one who had all the problems, all the responsibilities, all the dead ends and going nowheres. It was a new me who stepped off that coach, someone who was emptied of all emotion. I had no fear and no guilt and no hate and no love. The only way I can describe it is, imagine if you suddenly woke up one day and all your debts had disappeared and you had no one to answer to and no job to traumatize you and no people to persecute you. Imagine that all the normal rules of life were gone and didn't apply any more – you'd been cut loose from everything and were free. *Really* free! It was a kind of social suicide, I suppose. I'd decided – or something had decided for me – that I didn't want to be part of society any more. It was a primal feeling, running on instinct.

I asked at the Birmingham ticket office if there was anywhere I could stay for the night. They directed me to the pub across the road, which was called the Bull's Head. Fear filled me for a brief instant when I walked out of the bus depot. This was so precarious, almost sacrificial. I felt what the newborn must feel when it's hurled out into the world from the protecting womb-warmth. It gave an edge to my senses, but the trepidation went as quickly as it came. I was alive. Alert. Adrenaline rushed through my veins and my skin tingled. I was no longer myself, so I could no longer explain myself. There was nothing to explain. I forgot who I was, what I was, and every step became its own little lifetime – birth and life and death – and again – and again – over and over as I walked towards transformation.

The change was almost surreal, from what I had been in London just a few hours previously, to what I was now. I should have been worried and feeling guilty about the anxiety my family would be suffering, what I was putting them through, not knowing where I was or what had happened to me. I realize now how terrible the not-knowing is, how the not-knowing is the worst thing about someone going missing and how cruel it is to leave people like that. But how could I let them know? They would have come after me, traced me, found me and brought me back. It wasn't like I hated my family; I didn't – I'd just become numb and devoid of feeling for them. Any normal person in their right mind would think about the pain they were causing a family who loved them, but I wasn't in my right mind. I was someone else and in someone else's mind. I hadn't decided who that someone was yet, but I could be anyone I wanted to be – couldn't I?

It was about 5.30 p.m. and I felt revived, like I was embarking on a new adventure. The Bull's Head looked a bit dilapidated and intimidating to me and I wasn't sure about going inside. I found pubs daunting from my experience of them in my younger days, with Dad and Nan and my uncles. But I forced myself through the door. It was a noisy place, rowdy and full of drunks and dregs and pickpockets and pushers and slimy shysters. I could hear people walking up and down the stairs and it was like the walls were made of paper and had ears of their own. I should have been scared, but I wasn't. There was a growing feeling that I could take on the whole world. I can only explain it as bordering on euphoria and I'm sure it wasn't normal to feel like that.

The room they gave me for the night was large, with old brown well-worn furniture – 70s retro. It had a single bed and I didn't want to think about who'd slept in it before me, who'd cried in it or died in it. So I slept on top of the covers, fully clothed. I didn't trust the lock on the door and, if anyone was going to come into the room that night, as least I was going to be fully dressed. Thoughts of Nan and my dad came into my head, but I pushed them away. I'd walked to the edge of the cliff and jumped off – there was no going back now. I couldn't let those thoughts shake their accusing fingers at me. I didn't have the mental strength to face the repercussions of all the things I'd done wrong. I just couldn't handle it. Now the worry was gone, left lying on the road between London and Birmingham, and I didn't want it back again.

I slept well that night, in my little bed-and-breakfast room. I had no dreams and no shaking and no panic. My mind just shut down and for the first time in two years I had a peaceful night's sleep.

And I never touched Prozac again.

When I woke the next morning, I was disorientated for a few moments. I didn't really know where I was. Then I realized that yesterday had really happened and it was like I went into shock for a while. I just couldn't believe I'd left like that. Where did I get the strength from? Because that's how it seemed to me: I needed strength to do what I did, not cowardice. It was like I was running *to* something rather than running away. To try and forget the past, I decided to concentrate on the future, on what I needed to do. But first I had to move on from here. I was too close to the coaches. I knew my family and their friends would be checking everywhere – hospitals and police stations and train terminals and coach depots. Sooner or later they'd find the ticket woman with the greyish teeth and she'd remember an idiot girl who didn't know where she wanted to go, so she sold her a ticket to Birmingham. It wouldn't take them too long to find me if I was staying in a pub opposite the coach station.

I washed and dressed and left the room to go out and see what my new world was all about. I had very little money left, after paying twenty pounds for the room for the night. The Bull's Head was just down the road from Birmingham city centre, so I made my way up towards the High Street. It was very warm that morning and I was carrying the coat I brought from London with me. The only other clothes I had were the ones I stood up in. I probably looked a bit strange carrying the coat, but I had nowhere to leave it as I had to be out of the bed and breakfast by 10.00 a.m. The sun was milky overhead, trying to break through the thin cloud cover, and the light was translucent, like in a dreamscape, with everything in the foreground in sharp focus and the distant vista hazy, with soft outlines. I was moving slowly up a long hill and not concentrating on anything in particular. The city centre was being rebuilt and all I could see was scaffolding. I thought perhaps it was prophetic: a new life and a new city. I could see posts coming out of the ground underneath the scaffolding, like new shoots after a forest has been destroyed by fire. I was just in the moment, not realizing I'd need somewhere to stay that night, not even worrying about what the next hour or minute would bring.

Then a convertible sports car came round the one-way system and pulled up at the kerb beside me. The driver was older than me, with dark hair and eyes – a man with that ambient sense of hazard that some men have, men that a woman knows she should stay away from but is drawn to like a moth to a flame. He was holding a bunch of flowers. He didn't say anything, just reached out the flowers to me, and it was all part of the mirage, the ineffable moment, the unreality of it all. So I smiled and took them. The traffic behind was becoming irritable and horn-beeping, so he drove away and I waved goodbye and the flowers nodded their glorious heads in approval. I felt so utterly at one with everything.

I spent the next six hours drifting around town, trying to get my bearings and tentatively looking for a job. I went into the shops slowly, asking if there were any vacancies and holding the flowers in my hand. They must have thought I was on drugs or something and, in a way, I was – the drug of freedom. Mostly they shook their heads and smiled in a very suspicious way, but in Bay Trading the manageress was very taken with my calm and courteous demeanour and I got taken on as a store assistant. She asked me to start in three days' time.

I decided to buy a street map from somewhere, so I'd know how to get to places I might need to go and, when I turned the next corner, there was the flower man. I was alarmed at first. I didn't want to get to know anyone yet, having just escaped from an overpowering relationship with my family. But it was the way it happened, like it was kismet or karma, and I thought maybe this was all meant to be. I told him I'd only just arrived from London, having split from a violent boyfriend, and I didn't know anyone in Birmingham or have a job or any money, so it wasn't a good time for me right then. I shouldn't have said that – made myself out to be so vulnerable – but I was sure he'd think I was a vagrant and go away.

He didn't.

He persuaded me to let him buy me dinner and we went to a nice restaurant and he was light-hearted and easy to talk to. I couldn't eat much because my body had been rejecting food during my breakdown, making me throw up or giving me diarrhoea, and the sight of it normally made me feel sick. But we talked and laughed a little and he seemed nice and it was obvious that he was attracted to me.

He asked me if I had somewhere to stay and it was the first time I'd even thought about what I was going to do that night.

'No, I haven't.'

'We could get a room.'

'A room?'

'In a hotel.'

'We?'

It was then that his mobile rang and he spoke to someone on the other end and told them he was working. That's when I got suspicious. There was no wedding ring on his finger, but anyone can take a ring off, can't they! And instead of being light-hearted and easy and nice, he suddenly seemed dark and ugly and ominous.

'Are you married?'

'No.'

'Who was that?'

'My mother.'

It was such a blatant lie and he smiled when he was telling it, like it was something he'd practised and was very proud of. I waited until he went to the toilet, then I grabbed my coat and ran through the door, hoping by the time he came back it would be too late for him to follow me. I ran along the streets, turning one corner after another until I thought it was safe enough to stop. By then I was totally disorientated and lost, and it was late and the dark of the unfamiliar Midlands night was starting to intimidate me.

As I was passing a lighted telephone box, I thought about sheltering in there until it got light again. But what if somebody came to use the phone, or some drunk wanted a place to urinate? Then I noticed a card with the word 'SHELTER' on it and an emergency number to ring. I called it.

'Hello . . .'

'Hello.'

'I have nowhere to go.'

'Where are you now?'

'I don't know.'

The voice was kind and helpful and it told me to look for a street name and I did. Then I said I'd walked out of my old life and didn't want to go back. The voice was very understanding and didn't try to pry or ask me why. It wasn't condescending or patronizing and didn't ask for reasons or explanations that I didn't feel like offering. I'd blocked everything out and wanted it to stay like that. The voice was sensitive and soulful and just wanted to ensure my safety.

I was on the phone for a long time and the voice eventually found me a refuge for women in some obscure area of Birmingham. It asked if I had enough money for a bus, which I had, and it gave me directions how to get there from the phone box.

The bus ride took about fifteen minutes and my first impressions of Birmingham changed. The hopeful city with new shoots disappeared and was replaced by seedy streets and rundown areas of depression and decline. The part of the town I was heading into looked old and dirty and worn out, and my initial enthusiasm from the morning faded. The bus itself was very clean and very empty, which was strange to me. Buses in London were always crowded, but this one was exuberant in its newness and contrasted sharply with the scowling landscape outside its windows. Then the view from the bus changed again and the area we were passing through became very Asian in ethnicity, like Brick Lane or Southall in London. There were rows and rows of Asian shops and it felt exotic and slightly alien to me, as if I was no longer in England at all, but some more sensual country of brighter colour and elusive essence and smoky spiciness.

I thought about the incident in the restaurant and I began to understand the power of physical attraction for the first time. Oh, I'd attracted attention in the past, but my family had always acted as a shield to reflect it away from me before it could affect me in any serious way. Now it was mine and I could use it if I needed to. In the bank, I'd always been very businesslike and never even considered the idea of having to use anything other than my brain and my ability to get me where I wanted to go. To me, at that time, anything else would have been selling myself short. But now I had nothing left apart from the way I looked and I realized I might have to rely on that asset – the power of physical attraction – in the coming weeks and months.

I had to search for a long time to find the refuge. At first I thought I must have the wrong address because I couldn't find a door, only shop windows. Then I noticed there was a concealed entrance to the side of a nursery and I realized that women must come to this place who are in fear for their lives, so you couldn't have a neon sign saying 'WOMEN'S REFUGE' over the door. I pressed the buzzer and a support worker opened it. She'd been told I was coming and she greeted me warmly. She took me to a reception room and explained all about the refuge and its strict rules and regulations, and she asked me to fill out some forms with my name and address. I looked at them and wondered what I should write, then scribbled *Shelley Mackenney*, even though I knew that person was gone and I wasn't her any more. It was a mistake that would come back to bite me.

'I don't have an address.'

'Where were you previously?'

'Nowhere . . . on the streets.'

'Just put down this address, then.'

I knew if my family couldn't trace me through the train and coach stations, they'd believe I'd been kidnapped or murdered, and by now I was thinking that at least I owed it to them to let them know I was all right. I said as much to the refuge staff and they suggested I get in contact with Missing People, which was an independent charity connected to the police and funded by donations, for people left behind when someone disappears. I could get them to tell my family I wasn't dead or having my fingernails pulled out in some south London lock-up. But that would be all. Nothing else. No contact or crying or ranting or recriminations.

Next to the reception was the staff sleeping area, where a support worker stayed on duty twenty-four hours a day.

There was a large staircase to the left, leading to the first floor, which had a big double kitchen with cookers and fridges and sinks. Opposite the kitchen was a large communal lounge area with sofas and a big television set and tables and chairs, and, further along the corridor, I could see rooms to the left and right, including two shower/bathrooms and three toilets. Electronic fire doors dotted themselves at intervals along the corridor and they would close automatically if a member of staff pressed a button in case of emergencies. At the end of that corridor was a slim staircase leading up to the attic floor.

The room they gave me was a kind of garret at the top of the building. It was very basic, with a bed and a washbasin and a small television set. Everything else, like lounge, kitchen and bathroom, was communal. But it was like a little luxury apartment to me – all for myself with no intrusions and no traumas and no demons.

And I sighed with satisfaction.

4

The Refuge

For security reasons, I can't say where it was, but the refuge was a 'safe house' situated in an outlying area of Birmingham. When I first approached it from a distance, it looked like any other row of shops with flats above them, but, when I got closer, I saw it was a 'stay & play' nursery with children's pictures and their little projects in the windows. The entrance to the nursery was through the main doors, but there was what looked like a small alleyway to the right, with a large metal security door at the end of it. There was no number on the door, just an intercom and a CCTV camera pointing straight at it. Being next to the nursery, I suppose it wouldn't attract attention with women and children coming and going all day long. It was staffed twenty-four hours a day and the main door was closed and locked at 10.30 p.m. After that, no one was allowed in or out. There were ten bedrooms on three floors. The attic floor where they put me had only one other room and it was empty when I arrived, so I had the floor to myself. That suited me fine. I didn't really want to talk to anyone or get to know them or their problems.

It was a nondescript little room, with bare magnolia walls and a chintz cover on the single bed. Apart from the washbasin and the small TV, mounted high up on the wall, there was a mirror and that was it. A window over-looked the back garden, which was hidden from the outside world and full of toys and children playing. It seemed so tranquil, not at all what I would have expected a refuge to be like. I imagined a type of bedlam place, with fighting and screaming and people being dragged into cell-like rooms, but it wasn't like that – at least, not to begin with. The staff at the refuge were very good to me, making sure I settled in properly. I'm sure they thought I was on drugs of some kind, because the adrenaline rush and euphoria I felt meant I couldn't sit still. I was up early every morning and out all day exploring my new world. They never saw me eat anything – food was the last thing on my mind – and when I was in, I cleaned incessantly and tidied up, even though there wasn't much to clean or tidy. I showered and shifted about the room and stood up and sat down and couldn't settle in one single spot for even a second – anything really, so I didn't have to think.

These were the symptoms of post-traumatic stress dis-order coming out in strange ways. I didn't know that and, even though I was surrounded by support staff, they didn't recognize that I needed some kind of counselling either. Which surprises me, now that I've come through it – I can instantly see it in others and I would love to be able to do something to help people who've been through trauma in their lives. I have great respect for the volunteers and vari-ous organizations who are out there on the edge, helping people to rebuild themselves.

There was only one problem with the refuge. At the other side of the little alley another converted shop was situated. But this one had all the windows painted black and a bright pink neon sign over the door saying MAS-SAGE PARLOUR. The local newsagent's was straight across the road and the girls from the refuge used it for everything – as did the girls from the massage parlour. So the men loitering about outside made no distinction between the two and we were all fair game to them. Now, I was a little naive when I first got there from London and I thought the place was a genuine massage parlour. I mean, prostitution was illegal, so how could a brothel be operating openly on the street? I was enlightened one night when I went into a fast-food place a few doors down. One of the massage girls was in there and we got talking and she offered me a job. I was interested at first, until she started talking about the rates for hand jobs and blow jobs and full sex, and I ran out of there quickly without my chicken and chips.

I was in the refuge for about three months, waiting to be housed – and all that time women were coming and going, as if through a revolving door. Disillusioned, damaged, drugged – 'dregs', society would have called them, but they were eminently human in their wants and weaknesses and their pain and exploitation.

One very young girl came in – she was maybe only about sixteen. I don't know why she was there, but she had no contact with her mother and was being looked after by her father. The girl was really incapable, I mean she couldn't even boil an egg. Her father had only taught her how to deep fry chips and that's what she ate every single day. She was overweight and didn't have a lot of confidence. But she did have a lot to say, and in a very belligerent way – defensive, like a child who uses its self-hatred as a sword. When I got talking to her, I discovered she had a Kosovan boyfriend. He was much older than her and she'd go out with him every evening, and I found out he'd take her away in his car and she'd have sex with his 'friends' to please him. I told her she shouldn't be doing this and he was just using her and probably making money out of her as well. She wouldn't listen to me. She was hopelessly in love with him and she believed he loved her.

'You don't have to live like this, Zena.'

'I want to live like this.'

'There are better ways . . .'

'Why should I listen to you? Why are you in here?'

And she was right. There was no reason for her to listen to me, I was hardly a role model for anyone. It eventually started causing problems at the refuge because she'd return at all hours of the early morning and try to get in. I was afraid the support workers would think she was being deliberately troublesome and throw her out, so I told them what was really happening. But nothing changed. Because Zena was so young, she wasn't eligible to get a flat of her own; she'd have to stay in the refuge, or some other hostel, until she was eighteen. She'd have nowhere else to go if they threw her out – except into the exploiting arms of her so-called boyfriend. She disappeared after a while and I often wonder what became of her – it makes me feel so sad.

I suppose you could say that's where the refuge failed the women who came there for shelter from the brutality of their lives. It was probably due to the lack of resources, but they didn't have time to really get to know the girls, to get to know what was happening to them outside the refuge and to resolve the issues that brought them in there in the first place.

All the women who came in were damaged in one way or another. Most of them had suffered from physical and emotional abuse – violence and molestation and psychological exploitation and even torture – or they'd been through a series of 'carers' who didn't really care at all, who just did it for the money. A lot of them had mental-health issues and had led really horrific lives, and they came to the refuge to get away and try to recover. It was a place where they could try to build a new life for themselves. But the odds were stacked against them. They were constantly battling their own demons, the memories of their abuse, and they needed more than a physical place to go. They were lost and they needed a hand to lead them into the light of self-appreciation, away from the self-disgust that had been branded inside them by their oppressors. I saw them going out with man after man, desperate to find some lasting relationship, some lifebelt to cling to in a sea of sorrow. The support workers helped in practical ways, like showing people where to shop and how to budget their bills and how to manage their money and buckle up their belts. But there was no counselling, no emotional support, no one to wash the blood from their faces and the tears from their cheeks – and that's what was needed most of all.

You can't just take someone who's been through hell and give them a little space of their own and expect them to get on with it. They're emotionally exhausted and need to rebuild themselves. Unlike me, they couldn't cope alone, so they hooked up with someone they thought would stand by them and give them that renewal. But, nine times out of ten, it was some man who'd identified how vulnerable they were and used them to get what he wanted, not what was good for the women. They gave them drugs and drink to lure them in, to get their trust and affection, and it was an entrapment – once a woman was in, she couldn't get back out again.

Over the course of my 'missing' time, I had everything offered to me: cocaine, cannabis, crystal meth, heroin, amphetamine, angel dust – everything! And all kinds of alcohol. But I suppose some of my family's caution must have rubbed off and I didn't want to get out of my head and be at the mercy of some maniac who was just waiting for me to become incapacitated so he could take advantage. There were vampires outside the walls of the refuge, eager to pick up these vulnerable women and abuse them. The worst part of it was, the victims were prepared to put up with it, because pain and abuse were all they'd ever known. I didn't drink and I didn't take drugs, in some part due to my family's over-protection, but in a way it was my salvation as it stopped me falling prey to the predators.

That's not to say I didn't get attacked and experience the violence. I did. I'd only been in the refuge a short time when I was walking back along a main road and a car pulled up beside me. A man rolled down the window and asked if I wanted a lift. I said no and started to walk on.

'Do you smoke?'

'I've got cigarettes, thank you.'

'I mean green. I got loads. You wanna smoke some green with me?'

I didn't answer, just kept walking. The car roared past me.

'Slag!'

This was to happen countless times. They'd kerb crawl up alongside me as I was walking, minding my own business, ask me if I wanted some green or cheese or budda or ice or smoke. And, when I declined, I'd be a bitch, a slag, a whore, a lesbian. They seemed to think that because I didn't want to have casual sex in return for their drugs, I was either gay or frigid.

What arrogance!

I'd been at the refuge for about a month when I went over to the newsagent's on the other side of the street to get some cigarettes. As I crossed to come back, I had to walk between two parked cars, one of which was a large silver Mercedes. I could see the security door to the refuge and was heading towards it when a middle-aged Asian man appeared out of nowhere in front of me. He started to push me backwards, talking to me as he did so, but I couldn't understand what he was saying. I tried to get past him, but he grabbed my arm and started pulling me back.

'I pay you. I pay you.'

It was obvious he thought I was a prostitute – or else I was easy meat, being a refuge girl – and I should have been frightened. Instead, I was really angry, to think some complete stranger could just walk up to me and assume he could buy me. I was fuming. He pulled hard on my arm and I stumbled and fell against the open door of the Mercedes. I was still on my feet, but my back was against the open door frame and he was trying to push me inside. Then I felt someone's arms coming from inside the car and going round my waist, trying to pull me in.

I was thinking, 'This is bad, this is really bad.' The man in front of me was trying to get a grip on my arms and the one in the car was trying to pull me in from behind. It was a good job my father taught me how to fight and how to take care of myself, so I wasn't the helpless little girl they thought I was. I knew they'd have to bend me to get me into the car, so I braced my legs as rigid as I could against the door frame. It was hurting a lot and I knew the longer this went on the more chance they'd have of pulling me in. I had to get rid of the one in front of me, who was still trying to grab my arms and stop me from moving about. I closed my right fist and swung it as hard as I could into the side of his face. It stunned him enough to make him drop his grip and stagger back a bit. Then I reached down to the hands round my waist and dug my nails in as far as I could, drawing blood. The hands relaxed their grip enough for me to break free. I ran as quickly as I could for the refuge and slammed the security door behind me.

I think the only reason I survived that attack was because I was so full of rage at these men who believed they had the right to abduct me and do whatever they had planned with me. What troubled me most was the fact that other women were walking past while this was happening and nobody tried to help me. They obviously thought, like the men, that I was a prostitute and deserved to be treated like that. They looked at me with disdain on their faces, like I was dirt. Or maybe they knew I was a refuge girl and, to them, that was the same thing as being a whore.

The incident made me harder and put me on my guard, which was just as well, because many similar encounters followed, where men would try to get hold of me. One night I was in a phone box close to the newsagent's, when a man came in behind me, pinned me to the side and started trying to kiss me. He was skinny and wearing a baseball hat, and he was high on something – he stank of sweat and sexual psychosis. Because he wasn't very big and because my adrenaline count shot up immediately, I managed to push him back out through the heavy phone box door. I was trying to get away from him and make it back across the road to the refuge when I felt a kick from behind me. I stumbled and almost fell, and he was going crazy, trying to get to me. I scrambled on my hands and scuffed knees out into the road, just avoiding being hit by a passing car. He wasn't inclined to follow me out into the traffic and I regained my feet and ran to the refuge door. I was so angry I grabbed a knife so I could go back out and stab him. The security doors slowed me down and, by the time I got back out, he was gone. Thankfully. But I saw men try it with other girls too and I even got involved sometimes to stop it happening. And nobody did anything about it, not the police, nor the council, nor any of the authorities.

These men would loiter around the place at night like a pack of rutting dogs. I could see the cars pulling up and there would be three or four of them in each one. I don't know if they knew it was a refuge, but they sometimes tried to get through the security door and threw stones at the upstairs windows to attract the attention of the women inside. If we had to go out for anything, they looked at us with lascivious eyes when we walked past, like we were pieces of meat.

It was just awful.

I'm not trying to say I was Joan of Arc or anything, far from it. But I'd seen so much extreme violence growing up that I wasn't as intimidated as maybe I should have been. I was also naive in the ways of sexual manipulation, and neither did I take drugs or drink alcohol. My problems were all of a psychological nature. So perhaps it was a combination of my immunity to violence, naivety and absence of intoxication that kept me isolated from what was going on around me. Perhaps that coalescence of circumstance built up a subliminal shield that inadvertently protected me from the worst of the wickedness. I don't know for sure, I can only surmise.

Unfortunately, all the girls weren't like me and some fell into the trap of being groomed and subdued. I tried to tell them, to explain that the men didn't really care about them and they didn't have to go with them – they didn't have to have sex with every undesirable just to please a man – but they wouldn't listen. They'd only known disappointment and abuse, and that's what they related to. It's what they understood, because it's all they'd ever known. And nobody really cared. When you drop out of society, you're not a real person any more. You're a liability, a lost cause, a waste of time and resources. The world keeps turning and people keep walking past even when the predators have you surrounded and want your blood.

When girls came into the refuge, they were given

material support in the form of a bed and the basic necessities of life, but they all needed something deeper – even myself, and I wasn't as vulnerable as a lot of them. We all needed someone to help us get to the root cause of our unhappiness. And we were all unhappy, even if we convinced ourselves we weren't.

After a while, it was getting too claustrophobic being on my own all the time. Thoughts were trying to break through – little pockets of repressed memory rose and burst like bubbles in my brain. I'd been keeping myself to myself, keeping everyone at arm's length and not talking much to the existing residents. I liked it in the beginning when it was all new, the solitude, the withdrawal, and I didn't need anyone to invade my island. But it started to get oppressive and obsessive, and I knew it wouldn't be good for me in the long run. When new girls came in, they had no family or friends for support and they really wanted to talk to someone, so I started communicating, slowly and tentatively. I was cautious and didn't want to get too close, but I needed some company to keep the phantoms of my family away.

I started my job at Bay Trading but I didn't get paid till the end of the month. All social services would give me was a £30 crisis loan, so I had to walk to work and back every day, a distance of two and a half miles. I walked it four times one day when I had to go back in the evening for a meeting. At lunchtimes, I'd just wander about town because I couldn't afford to eat. I found it difficult working with lots of immature girls who had no real problems to speak of, unlike the women in the refuge, but were forever moaning about this or that triviality. I was offended by their insouciance, by their ignorance of the tragedy invisibly playing out all around them.

Then the police came looking for me. My family had been bombarding them with calls and pressurizing their contacts in London, and everyone was feeling the heat. The Birmingham police knew where to find me because I'd given my real name when I asked Missing People to make contact for me after I first came to the refuge. My past was catching up with me and it was my own stupid fault because I'd left a trail and the police were able to follow that trail. They found me and asked me if I'd consider talking to my family, but I refused. They couldn't make me. I was distraught and I left the job that day and didn't go back, in case somebody from London came there looking for me.

After that, I was more careful and didn't tell anybody anything.

The incident brought my family back looming large in my mind and I went out with the other girls from the refuge for a diversion. We went to a club and they wanted me to drink, but I wouldn't. Then a couple of men came to talk to us. They were very free with their money and they were soon joined by other men, buying drinks and offering cocaine and Es and I didn't like what was happening. I loved to dance so I went to enjoy the music and left them all to it. I could see them from a distance getting more and more wasted as the night wore on. There was a big crowd of men round them now. One by one, the girls drifted away, some with men and some to other clubs, except for one girl who was left on her own with about eight or ten men round her. Next time I looked, she wasn't there – and neither were the men. I went to the Ladies to see if I could find her and I knew something was wrong when I saw a couple of the men from the bar standing outside the door. When I tried to pass, they started getting all frisky and I was angry at first, but realized I'd have to stay calm if I wanted to get past them. I smiled and said I needed to use the toilet, but I'd be back in a minute. So they let me in.

When I got inside, I saw the rest of the men all bunched round a cubicle at the end. I went down there and tried to push my way through them, and I was getting hands coming from everywhere. I could see the girl inside the cubicle with her knickers round her ankles, completely wasted. She couldn't stand or open her eyes and was sitting on the closed lid of the toilet, being held in place by one of the men. She was like a little rag doll, all floppy with her dress pulled up. It was awful. I couldn't leave her like that. I told them security was coming and I had to get her out of there. I said I'd get her coat and they could come back to our place with us. It worked. They left the toilet and I tried to revive her. I poured water on her and gave her a cigarette and I got her to stand and we walked out of the Ladies, me supporting her with her arm round my shoulder.

The men had moved away a bit because they believed security was on the way, but they were waiting for us all the same. I managed to attract the attention of a couple of bouncers and told them I needed them to stay with me until I got her into a cab, which they did. The men were watching us from the club and they were giving me the finger signs and the cut-throat signs and the gun-to-the-head signs and I hoped I never ran into them again. Or I'd be in big trouble.

When the girl finally came round, back at the refuge, she swore she hadn't drunk all that much and they must have spiked her. She didn't bother going to the police because it would have been a waste of time.

After I walked out of Bay Trading, I found out that it was against the unwritten rules of the refuge to work. The cost for a place at the refuge was £400 a week – the reason it was so high was because of the support staff being on site twenty-four hours a day. As long as I was on social security, the rent got paid. But if I went to work, I'd have to pay the rent myself and a lot of girls had fallen into arrears in the past and had to be evicted. It was all too much hassle for them, collecting rent and evicting people, on top of everything else. So it was better not to find a job. But I don't do well sitting still for too long, so I composed a CV for myself and was hoping to get some work I could keep hidden. I wanted to earn myself some proper money, maybe save enough to be able to rent privately. I went to the library every day to use their computer facilities and, while I was there, I checked out all the job vacancies.

Then I came across something that seemed perfect for me and I really wanted it. It was the position of letting negotiator for a housing association that specialized in providing sheltered accommodation for vulnerable people. The job entailed interviewing and vetting applicants and showing the available properties. It appealed to me so much and I believed I'd be just the person to do it.

If I did get the job, I hoped I could wing it with the refuge for a while, until I saved enough money to move out – and I'd have a place of my own and a decent job at the same time.

I applied for the position, but I had absolutely nothing to wear for the interview. I couldn't just turn up in the clothes I was wearing, because I looked like I was living on the street. I went to social security and the refuge support staff, but no one would give me any extra money. So I went looking round the charity shops to see if there was anything I could get on the cheap. After walking miles and searching every shop, I finally found a suit – it was dark blue with a pinstripe effect. It wasn't anything as elegant as I used to wear at the bank, but it was just about passable for the interview. However, it was fifteen pounds and I only had a fiver. I really needed that suit if I was going to stand any chance of getting the job I wanted so much. I didn't want to steal it, I really wanted to buy it, but I didn't have a choice – or so my conscience told me. Because it was a charity shop, I felt utterly ashamed and disgusted with myself. I really, really didn't want to steal it, but there was no other option open to me. So I took it into the changing room with a load of other clothes and I pinched it – and I felt like the lowest of the low. I'd always believed in living a straight life, and this was going against my very nature.

I went for the job, but didn't reveal my past. I had to sit a couple of tests and have a couple of assessments and I passed them all. Then I had to conduct a mock interview, as if I was letting a property to a potential tenant. I loved it! I was made for it! It took me back to my time at the bank – I was there again and everything was all right. I didn't owe any money and I wasn't going under and life was lovely. They said I'd done very well and they'd be in contact. I gave them my address, but didn't tell them it was a women's refuge. I was so excited that I told some of the girls when I got back. I wanted to work! I was so happy!

Later that week, a man came buzzing on the main security door. The support workers asked him who he was and what he wanted.

'I'm looking for Shelley. We were out together today.'

I knew that was a lie. I hadn't been out with anybody and I never gave my real name to people I met in town. He kept on –

'She works for the housing association.'

They sent the man away, but I was called into the office and given a warning. They reprimanded me for telling men where I was living.

'And you know what could happen if you're found to be working, Shelley.'

They went on to lecture me on the nature and purpose of the refuge and how I shouldn't take it for granted or abuse my place there. I found out later that it wasn't me the man was looking for, but another refuge girl. She'd used my name and spun him a story about where she pretended to work to impress him when they met. But no one would own up to it and I had to swallow the warning. Then came the biggest irony: I got the job with the housing association, but I couldn't accept it because they were keeping an eye on me now and I couldn't trust the other girls not to reveal the fact that I was working. If I got found out, I'd be charged full rent and eventually thrown out on to the street, and I couldn't risk that happening.

I was devastated. The little ordinary dream that had become so extraordinary for me had evaporated. Such a simple thing. A job I knew I'd like doing. Such a truant thing now. Unobtainable. And the sun that came up for me earlier in the week now went down again.

I didn't go for any more jobs after that.

What was the point?

5

Stripper

After the initial adrenaline rush of running away, the gloss of Birmingham started to wear off and I felt I didn't fit in there. I missed the familiarity of London and the sense of being where I belonged. I didn't miss the panic attacks and the dreadful dreams and the hopeless heartache, but I missed the comforting and cohesive oneness that hides in familiar things. I wanted to see if I could find myself somewhere to stay in London, somewhere like the Birmingham refuge. I decided to go down there and have a look round. I used all the money from my social security payment to buy a one-way train ticket, because I didn't think I'd be coming back, but I didn't tell the support workers – just in case.

I made the journey from New Street to Euston, but as soon as I got off the train I felt sick and dizzy. My heart was thumping like it was going to explode out of my chest and I started to feel paranoid, thinking that eyes were watching me from everywhere. I couldn't stay any longer than I had to. I was in a state of panic, petrified that I'd be spotted, that I'd be recognized. The unthinkable had become thinkable again. I realized then that I just couldn't come back to London. Ever. Birmingham wasn't perfect, but it was the freedom I'd found at the other side of fear – no matter how tenuous. I knew I had to go but I had no money to buy a ticket back. I waited for a crowd and crushed through in the middle of it to the train and hoped an inspector wouldn't get on. I was lucky and didn't get caught when I crushed out with the crowd at New Street.

I was so glad to get back, even to the misogynists and misanthropes. I tried to help the girls in the refuge as far as I could, but there was only so much I could do without putting myself in danger. I stopped going to that club after the incident in the ladies' toilet, in case I met any of the men who were giving me the killer signs from the doorway that night. I never gave my real name to anyone again and made up bogus identities, a different one every time. I even tried to get my national insurance number changed but, apart from police protection cases, that was impossible.

I remember one day I went to Sparkhill with some of the girls – one of them was moving out and had got a grant to buy furniture. I'd never been to that part of Birmingham before and there was a group of us with about four children in tow. Then they met some men they knew and that was the end of the furniture shopping. They decided they were going to a pub. I didn't like drinking at the best of times, much less in the middle of the day, so they left me and went off with the men. I got lost and was passing the pub later, after going round in circles for a bit, and I saw that one of the girls had left her pram outside with the baby in it asleep. I'd never had any ambition to be a mother but, if I ever was, I promised myself I'd never be a mother like that. And that was the contradiction of these women – they were vulnerable and considerate and felt the pain of others, but they would enter into this world of drink and drugs that provided a temporary escape and they didn't seem to understand that it would affect their children the way it had affected them.

The freedom I found was a curious mixture of exhilaration and melancholy – euphoric at times of high optimism and sad when the light got too bright and I had to close my eyes against its inaccessibility. These sound like the classic symptoms of bipolar disorder, but it wasn't bipolar. It was more complicated than that – it was sweet and sour – a screaming silence – difficult to explain or quantify. It was a rebirth, bringing with it all the pain and strangeness and uncertainty and awe and expectation that birth, any birth, brings with it. It was difficult for me to start my life all over again at twenty-two. I had only what I stood up in and I missed all the little things I'd taken for granted up to then. I'd left with nothing and very little money to buy anything with, and the benefit I received barely kept me alive.

When I got my first few pounds from social security, I bought essentials like underwear, toothpaste, soap and shampoo. I could forget about clothes and cigarettes, and even food. Apart from the suit I stole for the interview, the only clothes I had were the ones I wore out of London on that coach and they had to serve me day in and day out for weeks. I had no make-up or other toiletries and, for a woman who prided herself on her appearance and wore make-up every day, it was verging on degrading – I felt like a tramp. I used to go into the chemist's and use the samples and never bought anything because I couldn't afford to. They'd get to know me in one shop and give me the evil eye, so I'd move on to another one, until they too began to notice I wasn't buying anything. By the time I ran out of chemists, they'd forgotten about me in the first one and I started the rounds all over again. What I'm saying is, I would have liked to have been able to buy myself a few nice things.

I love to dance. I don't have to have a drink or take drugs. When I dance, I feel the music running through my whole body and it just takes me away with it. One of the refuge girls took me to a party one evening and I danced – and when I say danced, I mean really danced. I was lost in the music and the rhythm, and I forgot about everything except the symmetry inside me, and I was following that magical melody that's as close to religion as I can get – the sound of my soul trying to break free and fulfil itself in an eternal present, not in a past that never was or a future that would never be. Eventually, a man came up to me and broke into my concentration. He said he worked doing security for Spearmint Rhino in Birmingham.

'You dance good. You should go there, they're recruiting.'

'I'm not a stripper, thank you.'

'It's not exactly stripping, just showing a bit of flesh for the customers. You keep your knickers on. Real good money!'

'No thanks.'

'I could introduce you.'

I just walked away from him. But later it got me thinking, got my mind drifting back to that first day in Birmingham and my new awakening to the power of physical attraction. I really needed some nice clothes and some decent make-up and other things, and I could use my only asset to get them. I could do with a bit of money and if it was only dancing, in a kind of bikini – like at the beach – what was wrong with that?

I'd never even been inside a strip club before, never mind dancing in my underwear for the customers. Could I do something like that? I was practically starving and I'd lost loads of weight and my body was probably good enough. But could I take my clothes off for money? As I started thinking about the money, it grew large in my mind – and so did the images of what I could buy with that money. I felt a twinge of the old addiction. An echo. It called to me and whispered in my ear and tried to seduce me. I'd seen expensive cars pulling up outside that night-club whenever I went past. How good was the money? How much could I earn? The images in my head eventually overcame my common sense and I decided to go along and see what it was all about. I rang them and, yes, they were always on the lookout for new girls, and they invited me down. They told me to dress real nice and they'd show me round and introduce me to the other girls – provided I could dance.

'Of course I can dance.'

'Good. You should be fine, then.'

The first thing I needed was a dress – and I found the perfect one. It was full-length see-through stretch lace, with ornate sequinned flowers and swirls to cover the private areas, and it was slashed up the left thigh to the waist. The price tag was £195 and I couldn't possibly afford that. Never. Ever. So I decided to 'borrow' it for the occasion. It was too tight to wear out under my clothes, so I took it back from the changing room and deliberately knocked over the whole rail so the dresses went every-where. The assistants came running to pick them up and, in the confusion, I stuck it under my coat and walked out with it. I thought they'd seen me and I ran when I got out-side the door. But no one came after me. As I said before, I wasn't a thief and stealing went against everything I believed in up to then. I'd seen my family involved in crime and I didn't want to be part of it. But extreme pov-erty and necessity while I was missing drove me to do many things I'm not proud of. I wasn't proud of them then and I'm not proud of them now. But this story would be incomplete and mendacious if I didn't write about them and tell it as it really was.

I tried psyching myself up before I went down to the club. I told myself I could do it, it was easy, I was a great dancer and that's all it was – dancing. I wasn't selling myself. Maybe I'd have to expose a bit of flesh but it was no big deal. I'd be OK. I'd be fine! I wore the dress and borrowed a pair of six-inch stilettos from a girl in the ref-uge, and some make-up from another one, and did my hair as best I could. I looked better than I'd done in months. But I wasn't feeling it. As I walked there with my coat over my 'borrowed' lace dress, the doubts started to creep in. Do they touch you? Do they expect something more than that? How can you stop them if they go too far? Are they all old? I'd heard they had private rooms – what went on in there? I was imagining scenes of all sorts of debauchery and was talking myself out of it before I even got through the door.

I don't think I can do this!

I took a deep breath before I walked into the club. It

was dark and sudden and claustrophobic. To the left of me a girl was dancing on a podium and I watched her. She was just dancing to the music and I knew I could do that. A group of men was sitting round the podium, drinking and laughing, and it was all right until she started to strip off. I looked around the rest of the club and all the dancers were doing the same thing. My heart sank. The bar hostesses walked about with bunny tails and fishnets and the men – there was something about the way they were leering at the women that disgusted me. It was like they were in a shop, deciding whether to buy something or not, looking the girls all over, up and down. I'd done some bad things in my time, but I couldn't put myself on display like that in public. All those men looked like they had money and they knew it. They strutted around like they owned the world and that didn't work for me. I'm not saying the girls were doing anything wrong, they were just trying to earn a living and, if they had the nerve for it, then good luck to them. But I knew I wouldn't be able to do it. I wouldn't be able to let a man lay down money and expect me to take my clothes off and dance in front of him for it. This wasn't for me. I might have lost everything else, but I still had my dignity and that was something I wasn't going to sell. At least not yet!

I walked back out.

At the time, I was living on one mini pizza a day – it cost a pound for two. I was eating one every day and that's all I had. But being like that was better than offering my body up on a plate to the highest bidder. As soon as I got outside, I knew I'd made the right decision. The relief I felt overwhelmed me, just as if I'd come to the edge of a cliff and looked over into the abyss, then drawn back, just in time. Next day, I smuggled the lace dress back into the shop I'd 'borrowed' it from and hung it back on the hanger.

There were times when I doubted my judgement. Why couldn't I do the things other girls had no problem doing? I felt so different, like an outcast, a freak. Did I think I was better than everyone else? I was no better than any of these girls, worse than some – at least they had an excuse for ending up the way they did. They'd been raped and tortured and driven insane, and they had every right to try and snatch any little bit of happiness that life doled out to them, even if that happiness was misplaced. I was here because I'd spent more money than I earned, that's all – nothing to shout about, no big deal – and I'd cracked under the pressure I'd created for myself. So maybe I *should* go strip in front of men and drink with them and take drugs and lie on my back for them and not be such a wimp about it.

Why not?

And then I withdrew into myself again and the old feelings came back and I didn't know who I really was any more.

When I felt like that, felt myself sinking down again, I listened to the music in my mind and tried to bring myself back up. Music and dancing always took me away – away from Birmingham and London and my life and who I was and everything. Everything! It was my chosen method of escape. Others chose alcohol or drugs or both, or love, or any substitute for love they could find. I chose music and dancing. After the stripper incident, I felt more down than usual, so I went to a drum and bass dance at the Custard Factory arts and media centre. I went alone because I just wanted to dance, not drink or take drugs or attract any idiots – all of which tended to happen every time I went out anywhere with a group of girls. I was wearing combat trousers and a short top that I got from a jumble sale. I bought a bottle of orange juice when I went in and spent most of the time on the floor dancing.

I kept the bottle of juice close to me because I didn't want it getting spiked. But when I'm dancing I lose myself, I'm just out of this world, and meanwhile the bottle was on the floor. At some point in the evening, I started to feel strange, like I had extra energy – all the energy in the world – more energy than I'd ever had. I was dancing like a dervish; I couldn't stop. I got so hot and thirsty I decided to go to the toilet and splash water on my face. When I looked in the mirror, I was covered in sweat. My hair was saturated and stuck to my head and my trousers and top were soaked through. Then I started to get a pain in my chest, as if I'd been stabbed with a knife. It was awful and I knew something was wrong.

It was time to get out of there.

I don't remember how I got outside, but I was trying to make my way back to the refuge, which was over two miles away. The next thing I remember is lying on the ground – it was a grassy area close to a McDonald's burger bar and it was dark. I had a really nasty pain in my chest and that's probably what brought me round. I was curled up on my side with my legs drawn up in a foetal position, really only half conscious of my surroundings. Then I became aware of a man sitting on the grass close to me. I couldn't tell if he was old or young or black or white, but he was looking at me and he had his hand on my leg. When he saw I was awake, he leaned over me. I could smell the sourness of his breath and his eyes were narrow, hooded, like he was trying to hide them. I kicked him in the chest and started screaming, and he ran off. My memory is still a bit hazy about this because I'd been drugged with something and I was out of it. But I remember standing up and staggering to the street, which wasn't far away. There was a bus stop and I must have got myself there from the club, but then fallen over the low wooden fence on to the grass near the burger bar. The refuge was only up the road and I made my way there. The men outside the massage parlour kept their distance from me because they thought I was drunk and I might vomit on them, which I probably would have done if they'd come near me.

I got up to my room, collapsed on the bed and slept for eternity. When I finally woke up, I realized someone must have spiked my drink with an E or even several Es, because I'd been dancing non-stop and that must have caused the chest pains. I felt sick as a dog and couldn't get myself right for a couple of days.

It was just another of the catalogue of incidents that happened to me while I was at the refuge. But I still needed money badly and was all the time on the lookout for some hooky way of working that the support staff wouldn't need to know about. There was one girl in the refuge who always seemed to have plenty of money. I was in the kitchen with her shortly after getting spiked and I was saying how sick I was of always trying to make ends meet on the pittance I received because I couldn't get myself a job. She said she was working cash in hand, so the support workers would never be able to find out about it. I was interested.

'I get paid well and it's so easy.'

'What do you do?'

'I'm a service provider.'

That sounded all right to me.

'They're always looking for staff.'

She gave me an address and told me to just look smart and I'd be OK.

Next day, I went round to the place and it looked like any normal office in a nondescript building. I wore the same suit I'd worn to the sheltered housing interview and, after waiting for a few minutes, I was called in by a man wearing a shirt and tie and looking very respectable. He sat behind a desk and kept going on about how the work should be fun. I should think of it as fun that I'd be getting well paid for. So far so good. Then he said, most of the clients were lonely middle-aged men and I should have no concerns about safety issues. An alarm bell rang in my head. I'd be freelance, of course, and could charge £100 an hour and the agency fee would be 30 per cent. I was starting to get more than a bit worried at this point. He pressed a buzzer and a woman of about thirty came into the room. She asked me to stand up. So I did.

'Can you strip to your underwear, dear.'

'What?'

'Strip.'

'What for?'

'So I can make sure you're not doing drugs.'

'I'm not doing drugs!'

'I need to check.'

I felt like swearing at her, but I didn't. Instead, I asked the man what kind of a service provider this company was. He laughed.

'We're an escort agency.'

I left and slammed the door behind me.

I don't know what it was – I suppose because we were vulnerable women, living in a refuge – but everybody seemed to think we'd be prepared to do any kind of dangerous, seedy or illegal work they wanted us to. Another girl told me she was on to a 'wicked earner' and she needed my help. All I had to do was go into shops and buy stuff and pretend to be someone else. She must have thought I was stupid. I worked in a bank and I knew all about credit-card fraud. I wasn't going to be used and put up front so my face was on camera doing the dirty work.

At one point a very rich man, with more money than I could ever earn in my whole life, took a fancy to me and offered to pay me to stay with him for one night. It sounds all *Indecent Proposal*, but I'm sure he wasn't talking millions, even though he never said how much. I met him a few times in a shop I used to go into to have a look round, even though I couldn't afford to buy anything in there. We had the occasional cup of coffee together and I actually liked him, and might have been prepared to continue our tenuous relationship and get to know him better. But as soon as he came out with such an arrogant and presumptuous statement, I stopped him in mid-sentence.

'No thank you!'

And I stood up and walked out the door. It showed just

what he thought of me as a woman and I found it deeply offensive. He wasn't the only one: I was propositioned left, right and centre – but I couldn't be bought. I turned them all down. I didn't have much, but I had pride and self-respect, and I found it insulting that men could think, just because they had money, I was cheap enough to lie on my back for them as soon as they clicked their wealthy fingers. I never did one-night stands and I wasn't anybody's piece of meat – and no amount of money was going to change that.

But I had to get myself out of the refuge. I'd been there long enough and it was time to move on. Time to get a proper job and a place of my own and start living again like a normal human being, not some wretch to be manipulated and drugged and dragged about.

6

Abducted

It was about a month or so after I walked out of the strip club without performing when I started to get the feeling I was being followed. Being watched. Observed. I was worried at first, I thought my family might have hired a private detective or got one of their underworld friends to find me. I believed I was safe inside the refuge, they wouldn't be able to get to me while I was there, but I had to go out on to the streets and that's when I was vulnerable. I was all the time looking over my shoulder, nervous and jittery. But nothing happened and I put it down to my imagination and started to relax. Until one night when I was coming back from a charity shop a few streets away and a man pulled up alongside me in a newish-looking car. The automatic window glided down noiselessly.

'Hi.'

I kept walking, speeding up my step.

'Listen, I'm not a punter.'

'Good, because I'm not a whore.'

I started to half jog, but the car kept up with me at the kerbside.

'I saw you at the club.'

'What club?'

'Spearmint Rhino.'

He stuck his hand out through the window. It had a card in it.

'Just take a look.'

I took the card to get rid of him. It said he was a professional photographer. I stopped jogging and stood still, but well back from the car.

'What d'you want?'

'No . . . what do *you* want?'

I didn't know what he meant, but he made no attempt to get out or approach me. He explained through the window that he'd seen me at the club and it seemed to him I was looking for a job, but chickened out. That meant I needed money, otherwise I wouldn't have been there in the first place.

'Am I right?'

'What if you are?'

'I can help you.'

'How?'

'Why don't we go get a drink and talk about it?'

I was wary. Anyone could get a card printed up and I was still thinking he might have been hired by my family. I told him I didn't drink and didn't like pubs. He suggested a coffee then. There was a café across the street and it was crowded with people. He said I'd be safe in there if I was worried about him. So I agreed.

He parked the car outside the café and held the door open for me. We found a table in the middle of the crowded room and ordered two coffees. He was about thirty-five and handsome and well-dressed, but I was still on my guard – I didn't trust anyone. I looked at the card again.

'I'm not doing nude photos.'

'What's your name?'

'Sandra.'

'And where do you live, Sandra?'

'None of your business.'

I hadn't given them any personal information at Spearmint Rhino and I wasn't going to give him any either. He smiled disarmingly, took a sip of his coffee and looked at me carefully, like he was weighing up my potential.

'How old are you?'

'That's none of your business either.'

He laughed and scratched his head.

'You're not making it easy, are you?'

'Making what easy?'

'For me to help you.'

'To be honest, I don't think I want my picture taken, thanks all the same.'

I stood up to leave. He caught my arm – not aggressively, just enough to stop me.

'Just hear me out, please. If you don't like what I have to say, then OK, no worries.'

I sat back down. He explained that he was an agent as well as a photographer – I could check out the web addresses on his card, ring them up if I liked, confirm his credentials. He ordered some strudel for us and I began to relax a little. But I still didn't want my picture taken – God knows where it might end up or who would see it. That wasn't a problem, he reassured me, there were all different kinds of fashion photography – I was a good-looking girl and had nice legs and hair and teeth. I could get work modelling shoes or jewellery or hair products. No one would need to see my face. I could pick and choose what I wanted to do and the money was very good and cash-in-hand. It sounded perfect. And he was polite and well-spoken and I started to believe him.

If I didn't want my face photographed, I must have a good reason and he said it was none of his business – he didn't want to know. Fair enough. I asked him what he got out of it and he said a finder's fee.

'Look, I have a studio close by.'

'A what?'

'A studio. We could go take some promotional shots.'

'I don't think so.'

'Why not?'

There was no way I was going to go somewhere with a perfect stranger, no matter how polite and well-mannered he was. I told him I'd check out the card and give him a ring.

'Is that yours?'

'What?'

He pointed to a twenty-pound note lying on the floor, close to our table.

'No.'

'Pick it up . . . quick!'

I bent down and picked up the twenty. What a find! I put it into my bag, looking round to make sure no one had noticed. He smiled.

'See, I've already made you some money.'

We agreed that I should check him out and then give him a call if I was interested. He told me to finish my coffee and he'd give me a lift home. I said no thanks, I'd rather walk. I swallowed what was left in the cup – and it was then I started to feel dizzy. I dropped my bag on the floor and slumped over a little. I was still fairly lucid, but finding it difficult to move. A waitress came over.

'Is everything all right?'

'It's my girlfriend, she's had a little too much to drink.'

'Not . . . his . . . girlfr—'

'It's OK, miss, I'll take care of her.'

He picked up my bag and started to lift me from my chair. I could see the waitress was worried and she called the manageress across. I tried to speak again.

'Drug . . . he –'

'She's had too much vodka.'

He handed the waitress some money, more than the amount of the bill.

'Keep the change.'

I could still hear them talking around me, even though I couldn't speak myself. The manageress was alarmed.

'I'm calling the police.'

She left the table to do that and I was grateful. But, before anyone else could intervene, he dragged me out of the café and threw me into the back of his car. Nobody tried to stop him. I passed out.

I don't know how long I was unconscious but, when I came to, it was daylight and I was still in the back of the car. It took me a moment or two to realize where I was and what had happened. I looked out the window and saw that we were somewhere very remote – no buildings or people or any signs of civilization, just a kind of wilderness landscape. The same man was driving the car and we were going very fast – like my father used to drive when I was a girl. I still felt groggy and had to coax the words to come out of my mouth.

'Where am I?'

He didn't answer, just kept driving fast. I tried to shout.

'Where are you taking me?'

He still didn't answer. I tried the doors, but they were locked and I couldn't get out of the car – which I would have done if I could, even moving at high speed. I started kicking the back of the driver's seat.

'Let me out! Let me out!'

He glared at me in the rear-view mirror.

'Stop that!'

'Let me out!'

I kept kicking.

'If you don't stop, I'll come back there and sort you out!'

The way he said it, I knew he meant it, and I was feeling weak, too weak to fight him off if he did.

'I'll call the police.'

'How? You have no phone.'

'My family will be looking for me.'

He laughed that laugh of his again, only this time it wasn't handsome and pleasant, it was sneering and arrogant.

'No they won't, you're a runaway. Nobody knows where you are.'

I was really worried now. I'd been abducted. This was the other side of going missing – the bad side. If unscrupulous people found out, they knew they could pick you off the streets and no one would ever know. How many times did this happen? How many missing people were abducted and never made contact with their families again, because they couldn't?

'Are you going to kill me?'

'Of course not.'

'What then?'

'I told you, I'm gonna help you make money.'

I shut up and decided to conserve my energy and make a run for it when we got to wherever it was we were going. He kept talking, trying to reassure me.

'You said you wanted to come with me.'

'Where?'

'The Gulf . . . Dubai, or maybe Bahrain . . . Yemen even.'

'I didn't . . .'

'Be better than what you've been used to.'

He said that's where the real money was. That's why I was in Spearmint Rhino, wasn't it, to strip and earn money? I didn't remember saying I'd come with him anywhere, even to his studio. He told me I got drunk, but I knew that was a lie.

We turned off the road and down along a kind of tree-lined dirt track that seemed to go on forever. I thought of grabbing him from behind, but he might have had a knife or some other weapon and there was the risk he'd crash the car and we'd both be killed. I had the feeling that if he'd wanted to rape me, he'd have done it by now and I'd be tied up in some basement torture chamber with a gag in my mouth. When we finally came out of the trees, I could see a small petrol station up ahead. He drove up to it and stopped the car.

'Need some juice.'

He got out and filled up the tank, then went inside to pay. I quickly tried all the doors, but they were locked, like in a police car. I was panicking, trying to remember the tricks my father taught me about cars when I was young. The car we were in was a Ford Focus W reg. and I knew there was a button on the far right of the dashboard, next to the window on the driver's side, behind the steering wheel. It released the boot. But before doing that, I needed to find a way into the boot from the back seat. I pulled up the bottom seating area to expose the body of the car. I then felt along the top of the seat backs, until I found the release buttons that enabled the back rests to fold down into the car, exposing the escape route into the boot. Once that was done, I scrambled forward over the front seats and pressed the button on the dashboard, then climbed back again and over the back seats into the open boot.

I was out!

In less than a minute.

I scrambled for the treeline, then ran and ran and ran, until I could run no more. I expected to hear him coming behind me. But there was nothing, so I collapsed exhausted into the foliage. After resting for a few minutes and catching my breath, I trudged on – and on and on – through the woods. I lost all track of time, but the light was beginning to go, so night must have been approaching. Then I came out on to a road. It was only a small, two-lane byroad and there was no traffic on it.

I trudged on, trying to keep away from the road, in case he came after me. It was raining and I had no money as he had taken my bag. Even if I wanted to try hitchhiking, which I didn't, not a single vehicle passed me in either direction. It was dark when I came to a small petrol station, the same one as before – where I escaped from the car, but it was closed now. I'd been going round in circles. The toilets were open though and I found some half-eaten food in a bin close by. I slept in a bolted cubicle in the Ladies that night, out of the rain. I was going to wait until the petrol station opened next morning and call the police, but what if the owner was in on it with him? Maybe that's why he was in there so long. I'd seen that kind of thing in films, in remote parts of America – where girls thought they'd escaped, only to be dragged back by the very people they went to for help. I was in no-man's land. I had to get further away, so I left as dawn was breaking and trudged on until I came to a small town. I thought about going to the police there, but I had no idea where I'd come from and the police would want to know who I was and they wouldn't believe me and would send me back to London when they found out I was a missing person.

I suddenly remembered I'd been away from the refuge for two nights and the maximum they allowed was three – after that, if I didn't get back, I'd be thrown out. I kept moving, avoiding the town as best I could. The small roads merged with a bigger, trunk road, with a lot of traffic on it. There was nothing else for it, I had to hitchhike if I wanted to get back to the refuge in time – and I still didn't know how far away from Birmingham I was. It wasn't long before a big lorry pulled up. I was totally exhausted and thought a lorry would probably be safer than a private car. I climbed up into the cab.

'Where to, miss?'

'Birmingham?'

'I can take you as far as Bradford.'

'Thank you.'

It took him three hours to drive to Bradford, that's how far away I was. I fell asleep on the way and he woke me when we pulled into some motorway services.

'You want to get something to eat?'

I didn't realize how hungry I was. He bought me bacon and sausage and eggs and beans and fried bread, along with a big mug of tea, and I'll never forget that driver's kindness. God bless lorry drivers everywhere!

'What's your name?'

'Jodie.'

'I'm Bill.'

He held out his big hand and I shook it. He was about fifty, with a checked shirt like all lorry drivers wear and a peaked cap and a big heart.

'You were a long way from Birmingham, Jodie.'

'Yes. Visiting friends.'

'Did you hitchhike up?'

'No, went on the train. But my bag got stolen.'

'Wouldn't your friends help you out?'

'It was after I left, near the station.'

He could see I didn't want to talk about it, so he stopped asking questions and told me all about himself. But I wasn't really listening. I couldn't believe what had happened to me and what a lucky escape I'd had. I could have been on my way to some flesh market in Yemen or Qatar or Bahrain or Dubai if it wasn't for what my father taught me when I was young.

It was about 6.00 p.m. when the trucker dropped me off in Bradford. I thanked him and said goodbye. He told me to be careful. I was still over a hundred miles away from Birmingham, with no money, but I felt safer now for some reason. It was getting late and I didn't fancy hitch-hiking in the dark. I wandered round the city for a long time, not knowing what to do, but not wanting to sleep rough either. I decided to fall back on the power of phys-ical attraction, even though I must have looked a right sight after three days on the road without a wash. I found a pub that looked about right – not too rough and not too posh, with a dark alley running alongside it. I went to the Ladies and tidied myself up as best I could. The lights were subdued, so I didn't look as bad as I did in the day-light. I asked the barman for a glass of water.

'Still or sparkling?'

'Just out of the tap, please.'

'Will you be buying anything else?'

'Yes. I'm waiting for someone.'

He served me the water and I sat on a stool and waited. It wasn't too long before I was approached by a likely lad who was a bit inebriated and full of Dutch courage. He was short and skinny and he didn't look too threatening.

'I hate to see a lady drinking on her own.'

'Who says I'm a lady?'

'Aren't you?'

'And if I'm not?'

He looked around before answering me in an awkward, embarrassed voice.

'Eh . . . how much?'

'Fifty.'

'That's a lot of money.'

'I'm worth it.'

He hummed and hawed about it for a few minutes and I got off the stool.

'Where are you going?'

'To find someone else.'

'Wait!'

He drank back the rest of his beer and looked at me. Waiting. I looked back at him with a puzzled expression, not knowing the rules of the game.

'Well?'

'Well what?'

'Where to?'

The penny dropped. He expected me to have a room nearby. He wasn't going to give me fifty pounds for a knee-trembler up the alley.

'Just round the corner.'

We left the pub and I took him into the quiet and dark alleyway, not having a clue where I was going to go.

'Money up front.'

'I'll give you the money when we get there.'

'How do I know you got fifty on you? You might be wasting my time.'

'Oh, all right . . .'

He was a bit drunk, otherwise he wouldn't have parted with the cash so easily. We walked a bit further, through a maze of little backstreets, until we were totally lost.

'Where is this bloody place?'

'Almost there.'

'Wait!'

He went over to the wall and unzipped his trousers. That was my cue. I waited till he was in full flow and would find it difficult to stop without wetting himself, then I took off at a run.

'Hey! Come back!'

I zigzagged through the backstreets, hoping I wouldn't run up a blind alley. He came after me, but he couldn't move very fast and I soon outstripped him. I could hear him screaming in the growing distance between us.

'Slag! Bitch! Whore!'

By the time I found my way to the station, it was past midnight and the last train had already left. I spent the night on a bench, hoping no louts or lushes would come and try to molest me. But it was all quiet. An off-peak single to Birmingham cost £42 the next morning after 9.30 a.m. and I was able to afford it. I slept on the train going down and walked the rest of the way to the refuge when I got to Birmingham. The support workers wanted to know where I'd been and they were a bit cross because I hadn't told them I was going to be away for a while.

'I'm sorry. I went to see some friends.'

'You should have let us know, Shelley.'

'Yes, I know. I had no phone.'

'Didn't your friends have one?'

'Yes . . . I should have borrowed one. I'm sorry, I didn't think . . .'

They let me off on that occasion, because my attendance record at the refuge was so good, unlike a lot of the other girls.

But I was worried: the man who abducted me knew I

was a missing person and he'd been stalking me. What if he was still out there and came after me in case I went to the police? I couldn't take any chances. The next day I got one of the girls to cut my hair short and I dyed it blonde. I stole a pair of black-rimmed plain glass frames from a local optician's and I only went out when I absolutely had to. Over the next few weeks, nothing happened and I began to chill out. But I came to the conclusion that a missing girl on her own was fair game for any pervert or criminal. Two girls would be safer than one.

I had to make a friend.

7
Homeless

There was one girl I became quite friendly with after that. Her name was Alice and she had a child, a little girl of about three called Emily. Alice was from outside Birmingham, like me, and she had nobody, like me, so we hit it off when she came into the refuge. We made friends late one night when neither of us could sleep and we were both down in the living room, and we talked for hours. She'd had a rough life, seeing a lot of abuse as a child. Then she took up with a heroin addict who was violent and she had to get away from him for the safety of her child. You have to know this about women who've had hard lives and been abused: they're usually very kind and compassionate people – the harder their life, the kinder they are. Alice was generous and understanding and very emotional. She would give her last penny to a beggar, just so she knew he wouldn't go without. People who have led horrific lives seem to understand other people's pain; they feel for anyone who's suffering because they liken it to their own suffering. They will go out of their way to help, because they know what it's like to be so badly hurt. But Alice had another side – she could get very erratic and aggressive, and that was because of drugs.

She loved her little daughter.

But she was lost.

We got so close, she went around telling everybody she was my sister. We'd go into town every day and window shop. We never had any money, so we couldn't afford to buy anything, but it was nice to look and pretend. On one occasion, we were browsing through a bargain clothes shop when I saw a backless halter-neck catsuit. I really loved catsuits at the time, so I just had to try it on. When I came out of the changing room, Alice wasn't there, but I saw her across the street talking to some man. Emily was crying and I thought he might be giving her grief, so I rushed out of the shop and over to her. But it was nothing to worry about. She'd gone outside for a cigarette and caught the eye of this man, and she'd gone over to talk to him. She would do that, chat to men and smile at them if she thought they could give her what she wanted. And that made her vulnerable and put her at risk. But this time it was all nice and pleasant, no nasty stuff, and he asked her to go for a quick drink with him. He said he was on his lunch break and she asked if I'd look after Emily for an hour. I liked children, even though I never believed I'd have any of my own. So I agreed.

They went off and I started pushing little Emily along, chatting to her and trying to get her to stop crying, not paying much attention to anything else. About fifteen minutes later, I started to wonder why I was getting a lot of wolf whistles and woo-hoos and drawing the attention of the men who were passing. Then I realized I was wearing the catsuit and my other clothes were still in the changing cubicle of the shop. I didn't know what to do – if I went back there and tried to explain, they might not listen and accuse me of shoplifting, and then I'd get arrested and be thrown out of the refuge. But the catsuit was a little out of place at lunchtime in a shopping area and I was drawing smiles from the men and frowns from the women and whispers from behind the hands. I went somewhere quiet, but still couldn't settle Emily. An hour passed and Alice didn't appear. I tried to ring her from a phone box, but couldn't get an answer. I rang and rang and rang, and hours went by and I was getting really frustrated and annoyed. Her phone was eventually answered by the man she'd gone off with and he told me they were in a pub down the road.

I marched straight down there and gave her her daughter back, and I must have looked like that woman from *The Avengers* because I was really angry with her and she was a little intoxicated and everyone was staring at me. It reminded me of when I had to go into the pubs in London with Nan to find my dad and uncles. After I gave her Emily and a good mouthful of abuse, I stormed towards the door. On the way, a man approached me and asked if I was all right. He had an accent and looked foreign, Italian or Spanish maybe, with short black hair and a slight build. He smiled when he spoke to me and I remember thinking for a fleeting moment that he had beautiful green eyes. But I was so angry I just pushed him out of the way and he nearly fell over. I had to walk all the way back to the refuge in the catsuit, all through town and Digbeth and along the dual carriageway, with blokes whistling and calling out of their vans and lorries. I was glad to get in and didn't speak to Alice for a good while after.

Every time I went into town with the refuge girls we got involved with men. I don't know what it was with the women, most of them weren't overtly looking to get laid, but it must have seemed like that to the men they met. Maybe they were just seeking attention or love or their interpretation of what attention and love was – they had a very limited experience of either. But I wasn't. And I wasn't going to give it out to any idiot who flashed me a smile. So I usually ended up walking off on my own and the other girls didn't care. They had no sense of loyalty to me and why should they? They thought I was boring because I didn't like alcohol or pubs and, if I went to a club, I just wanted to dance.

But they should have had a sense of responsibility to their children, even if they had no respect for themselves, and this was something I could never understand. And still can't. On one particular day, the usual thing happened: the girls I was with attracted a group of men and one of them started to get all touchy-feely with me. I told him politely I wasn't interested in him and he went crazy, calling me a slag and a whore and a lesbian. I walked away, but he decided to follow me, still screaming and calling me all the names under the sun. He was quite scary-looking, tall and muscular, but after a while of this I'd had enough, so I turned round and faced him.

'You want to know why I'm not interested in you?'

'Yeah!'

'Because I'm not a slag like the rest of them. If I was, then I might be interested in you, because only a desperate slag would want to sleep with someone like you.'

He was stunned into silence and I walked away from him.

I made it up with Alice eventually and I loved little Emily so, when she made a date with the man she'd met in town and asked me to look after the child, I agreed to do it. I agreed even though it was prohibited by the rules of the refuge. Mothers staying there weren't allowed to let anyone else take care of their children. This was for the kids' protection, because all the women there had issues and problems of their own. I couldn't look after Emily in the refuge, so I had to take her outside to a park. Once again, Alice told me she'd only be out for an hour or so, but she didn't come back and the little girl was getting tired and hungry. I had no money and didn't know Birmingham very well, so the only place I could take her was back to the refuge. As soon as I came through the door, they saw that Alice wasn't with her child and they called social services. When Alice finally came back, after four or five hours, the support workers told her she couldn't stay at the refuge any longer because she'd broken the rules. She'd have to leave, and take Emily with her. I couldn't understand why they'd do this – if they cared for the welfare of the child, surely they couldn't just chuck her out on to the street? They gave Alice the address of another hostel that would be willing to take her in, so I went with her, even though the support workers at the refuge warned me not to get involved with her problems as it could jeopardize my own room there.

But the new hostel was a dreadful place. Gangs of crack cocaine addicts hung around outside and intimidated everyone going in and out. Alice would have to share a room that had bunk beds. The room was tiny, with no television, and they gave her one bowl, one spoon, one knife, one fork, one cup and one plate to use. It was like something out of a Charles Dickens novel – a workhouse or a spike or a house of correction.

'I can't stay here, Shelley.'

'You have to, Alice.'

'I can't!'

At the time, I was close to getting a one-bedroom flat in Birmingham and leaving the refuge. I was due to move into it in three or four weeks and I was trying to get a grant to furnish it.

'Listen, if you stick it here for a few weeks, you can come live with me in my flat.'

'I can't stay here for a few days, Shelley, never mind a few weeks.'

So she walked out, and now she was homeless. So was her little child. It wasn't really my problem, but I felt really bad about it and responsible in a way. I considered trying to smuggle them back to my room at the refuge so they could have somewhere to stay, but I'd never have got away with it – heavy security doors, twenty-four-hour personnel, CCTV – what could I do?

Personally, I was growing more confident in myself. I'd resisted all the attempts by men to take advantage of me and survived an abduction. I'd resisted the alcohol and the drugs and escaped the Gulf slave trade and I was confident I could handle any situation. I was bordering on euphoric at times, although this was a symptom of post-traumatic stress disorder and I just didn't know it. I wanted to live independently now and experience a better side of life. I knew some things still got me down, but I'd never again be dragged so far into the pit of darkness that I'd contemplate suicide like I did before. I'd never again allow depression to take over my soul to that extent. I'd carry on and nothing would stop me. I was so disappointed at losing everything in London and I was laying the blame for that at everyone else's door. I felt angry because no one saw the signs and no one came to help me. From now on I would rely on myself and I believed I could take on the whole world if I had to. It was a kind of madness – a false estimation of my own abilities. I could take on whatever came my way and I didn't need to worry about the consequences. So, when Alice was kicked out of the refuge, I decided to go with her. I didn't think she'd be able to cope on her own and I was worried about what might happen to Emily. I already knew the rules of the refuge stipulated I could only be absent for three nights in any one week or I'd lose my room. Apart from the time I got abducted, I had a good record and hadn't stayed out any other night in the three months I'd been there, so they knew I wasn't being difficult and they gave me some leeway.

The manager of the refuge called me into her office. She knew what I was doing and she advised me not to leave to go with Alice and Emily. She said it wasn't my problem and I shouldn't get involved. But I had to, I just felt like I had to. The manager gave me ten pounds out of her own purse and wished me luck, but told me I'd better be back in three days.

Or not at all.

I helped Alice to pack her few bits and pieces into black bin bags and it wasn't until we were out on the dark night-time street that I realized the full enormity of what I'd done. Here we were, her with her young child in her arms and me pushing her buggy with the bin bags. We were like a couple of hobos. Alice had just been paid her social security or child benefit, or whatever pittance it was the state gave her to exist on, so we walked to the nearest cheap hotel and paid forty pounds for a room for the night.

I'd never stayed in a hotel before and I didn't even know how to use the swipe card to open the door. It was a family room, when we eventually got inside with the help of a cleaner who looked at us like we were from Mars or something. It had a king-sized bed in the middle and a small pull-out bed at the side for Emily. There was a television, a shower, a toilet and washbasin, and, to be honest, I thought if I was homeless and had to stay somewhere, this place wasn't so bad. But there was no way we could afford £40 a night. This one night had nearly cleaned us out and we had to be gone by 10.00 a.m. next morning.

The next day, we went along to McDonald's, the one next to the grassy area where I'd fallen down that night my drink was spiked. We tried to plan how we were going to make £40 a day to pay for the room at the hotel for the next few weeks until my flat was ready. But the first thing we needed was food. We pooled our money together and bought a burger meal between us. After eating most of it, I pulled a hair from my head and stuck it into what was left of the burger. I then took it back to the counter and created a scene about the poor standard of hygiene in the place. They gave me my money back as a goodwill gesture and to get rid of me before I upset the other customers. So we went down the street and did the same thing at KFC – then at Burger King. We must have pulled this stroke in every fast-food place in Birmingham during the time we were homeless and on the streets.

That was the food taken care of. Next, we needed money for the hotel room. I rang social security from a phone box and told them I'd had my bag stolen with all my money in it and I had nothing to survive on. I had to ring the police as well and report the 'theft' to get a crime number. Once I had that, I went to the main social security office, signed a declaration and filled out an application for a crisis loan. I waited for three hours and, finally, they gave me a giro for £40. That paid for the hotel room for another night and I got Alice to do the same thing the next day, so we got a further night off the streets. But we couldn't do it any more after that, so we had to find other ways to make money.

The Small Heath area of Birmingham was full of young Asian men who were always on the lookout for a pretty face; all you had to do was flash a smile their way and they'd be queuing up. As much as it pained me to do it, there was no other option at that point in time. Finally, I had to use the power of attraction, the asset I'd been holding back in case of emergencies – for a rainy day. This was an emergency. And it was raining.

The first one I attracted was a young man of about twenty-three, driving a BMW. He pulled up beside me and started with his chat-up lines.

'Hey, beautiful, you want to come for a drink?'

I fluttered my eyelashes.

'I'd love to, but I'm homeless at the moment.'

'Homeless?'

'I've run away from my violent boyfriend. I had to leave everything behind. I have no family . . . nothing.'

'I can help you.'

That's exactly what I wanted to hear. I told him I needed a place to stay for myself and my young daughter, and he said he had a friend who had a place. That wasn't any good to me because I wanted the money for the hotel, not to stay in some stranger's house or flat – it would be too dangerous, especially with a child.

'I can't stay in some strange place with my daughter.'

A lot of these young men were very flash and they liked to give the impression they had lots of money and kudos – it was a testosterone thing.

'So, what do you want?'

I smiled, fluttered my eyelashes again.

'I know a cheap hotel.'

'How much is it?'

'Forty pounds.'

He gave me a funny look, like he was weighing up the proposition, taking stock of the situation, examining the alternatives.

'If you pay, then we can go for that drink.'

'Get in the car.'

I hesitated, not really knowing what I should do. He obviously wasn't going to hand me forty pounds, just like that, in case I ran off. So I took the chance and got into his car. I was still trying to be all nice, pretending that I was interested in him.

He gave me the forty pounds and I was all eyes and teeth, really excited and giving him the impression I was so grateful and really wanted to go somewhere with him. In reality, I *hated* doing it! It's painful to even think about it now and I've had a big problem writing this chapter, because it's something I'd rather forget about. But it's part of the story, so it has to be told. I also have to say this: I only conned what I needed to, never to have a good time or earn a lot of money, like some. I did it because I had to and because there was a child involved, who needed food and shelter, and other things as well. But I really did despise having to con these men out of money, having to use the power of physical attraction. It placed me in some dangerous situations and I stopped doing it as soon as I could. I just want to make that crystal clear.

'It's a beautiful car.'

'You want to drive it?'

'Could I?'

'Sure.'

We switched seats and I drove the car around for a bit. His hand was roving over my leg as we went and I was starting to get a bit nervous, but kept smiling. He directed me to an Indian fast-food place in Small Heath. I was just waiting for my chance to jump out the door as soon as I could, but it was difficult with me driving and I wondered if he'd done that deliberately. To my surprise, he asked me what I wanted to eat and he went into the shop to get the food. I was out and gone while he was in there – and I had enough for another night at the hotel. I estimated that, when we left the refuge, there was a total of twenty-five days until I got my flat – twenty-five days and twenty-five nights. This was night four taken care of, with twenty-one to go. I made my way to the hotel, down the backstreets. I hated what I'd done and I was shaking. It felt wrong, but I had to continue.

All the 'target' men were young Asians and they lived either with their mothers or with their wives. They rarely lived alone, so they were unlikely to take me back to their place, which was good for me. The first time, I was nervous and hesitant, but I began to get used to it as the days went by, going to a different area each time to avoid the chance of being seen by someone I'd already taken money from. I'd escaped abduction and made my way back from the brink of nowhere with nothing, but I was still nervous that I'd be walking down the street one day and someone would come up behind me and I'd be in deep trouble again. The routine of pretending I was interested in these men wasn't sitting right with me either and, once I got the money, I couldn't wait to get away from them.

We still had about sixteen nights left in front of us when I was stopped by a man while I was out on my 'patrol'. There was something different about him – he wasn't trying to impress me with his patter and his chatter. He was *really* a hard nut and I'd seen a few of them in my younger days. Despite my disquiet, I went through the routine and he offered to help me, but he wanted something in return. And it wasn't sex. He asked me to go to a club and find a certain man there. Then I was to get close to that man and get him to take me home with him. Once inside his place, I was to call a number and let some people in when they arrived.

'I'll pay you five hundred pounds.'

My jaw dropped. That kind of money would solve most of our problems and I wouldn't have to do this again. No more power of physical attraction. No more streetwalking.

'Who's the man?'

'You don't need to know.'

'Yes, I do.'

He was a drug dealer and these people wanted to get inside his house to do him over and take his money and his supply. I was tempted, I really was. But my instincts told me not to do it. All right, I wouldn't have to walk the streets again, but to go to a strange place with a drug dealer and, if he didn't rape me first, let a gang of thugs in to seriously hurt him, then hope the dealer never saw me again – not to mention being an accessory to assault and robbery in the eyes of the law. No! This was like going back to the bad old days of London. This was what I'd always hated – serious crime, serious violence – and I wasn't going to go down that dirty road.

I walked away.

I heard later that another refuge girl did it and she was found wandering about in a traumatized state, covered in blood. Somebody said she'd been sexually assaulted and had her face slashed with a Stanley knife.

I started 'patrolling' around the Coventry Road area of Birmingham and I'd get the men to take me to the McDonald's burger bar, close to the hotel. As soon as I got the opportunity, I'd slip away and sneak into the hotel, and that lessened the chance of them following me and picking me up off the street as I tried to make my escape. I used different names every time; that way, if someone did call after me down the street, I wouldn't turn round to be recognized. I got so adept I was able to read their personalities as soon as they started talking to me – what they would be like, if they were aggressive, if they'd try to take what they wanted, if they were just showing off. I always trusted my instincts and walked away if I thought the man was a high-risk prospect.

Then there was the cheap hotel itself. I came down late one night to find out something, I can't remember what. I went to reception but it was closed. I heard voices coming from the bar, and I went in there and found the night porter with a couple of men. They were all a bit merry and chatty, and I hung around for a while, sizing up the situation. I told them I had to go see to my child, but not before I'd searched their coat pockets and stolen about sixty pounds – another night's shelter and some stuff for Emily.

While I was doing all this, Alice was taking care of Emily, but she was also chasing the drink and the weed and one day, when I returned, I found her in the room with about five men, all smoking marijuana. I was furious, because I was trying to use my talents to survive, without having to give away too much, and she was just making a mockery of it all. The men were lying on the bed and making themselves at home. I tried to get them to leave, but they weren't going anywhere until they'd got what they mistakenly believed they'd come for. I went down to reception and reported them. I said they'd just turned up at the room and we couldn't get rid of them. Security came up and there was a big fight, with things getting smashed and Emily crying. The men were thrown out — and us after them.

We'd lost our cheap hotel room.

And we still had nine nights to go.

8

The Streets

It was the middle of the night when we were thrown out of the hotel and it was raining. We had no money and nowhere to go. All the hostels were closed for the night by then and wouldn't open their doors to us. We sheltered in a phone box and Emily was tired and crying. Unlike me, Alice still had contact with her mother. She didn't want to do it, but I made her ring home. We couldn't keep Emily out on the streets all night and if the police came along, they'd get social services involved and she'd be taken away from Alice and probably put into care. Already we were attracting the attention of drunks and drug addicts and all kinds of weird predatory shadows slinking in the dark drizzle. Alice's mother lived in Tamworth, or somewhere like that, and she didn't get on with her daughter. I was told she was on opium while Alice was growing up and she'd allowed her daughter to be molested by men. Alice's stepfather was a manic depressive and he used to lock her in a garden shed and forget about her.

In many ways, Alice was a lovely, kind person, but she could consume a lot of alcohol and drugs in order to forget her past and try to forgive her mother, and she never seemed able to do either. Now the time had come for her to let go of her bad memories for Emily's sake, at least for the next nine nights. The mother could hear the little girl crying and that melted her hard heart enough for her to agree to drive into Birmingham to pick up her daughter and granddaughter and shelter them, at least for a while.

'There's someone with me, Mum.'

I couldn't hear what the woman was saying on the other end of the phone, but I knew it wasn't good.

'She's not a drug addict, Mum.'

Alice was pleading.

'Please, Mum . . .'

Then the phone went dead. Alice looked at the receiver and hung up. Her face said it all.

'She won't take you in, Shelley, just me and Emily.'

'It's OK, Alice. I'll be OK.'

'I won't go, I'll stay with you.'

'Don't be stupid, you have to go with Emily.'

Alice hugged me and I hugged her back. For all her faults, I'd formed a bond with this unhappy woman and we were the closest thing to family that either of us had.

'How . . . how will you be OK, Shelley?'

'I'll find another cheap hotel, don't worry.'

About an hour later, a car came and took Alice and Emily away. I watched from the wet phone box. Alice looked back at me through the window as they drove off and gave a little hopeful wave.

I was alone.

It was too late and too dangerous to try to find someone to con out of the price of a room and then find a new hotel to take me in. I'd just have to doss down somewhere for the night and get my bearings in the morning when it was light. There were places where homeless people sheltered near the city centre and close to where I was, the alleys on Broad Street or the subways under Five Ways roundabout. I thought somewhere like that would be better than staying in the lit phone box with all the ghouls circling in the darkness outside. It would be only a matter of time before they invited themselves in. I pulled up my hood and hunched my shoulders and made out like I was one of these lost souls, shuffling my way along the dingy streets. It was raining harder now, and cold, and I just wanted to find somewhere dry – somewhere I could sit down and sleep.

I found a doorway down some side street that was sheltered and there was heat coming out from under the door. It must have been a restaurant or a café or fast-food place and I didn't care because I was exhausted from the hassle of the day. I found a kind of waterproof tarpaulin thing lying close to the wall and I pulled it over me and closed my eyes.

It was still dark and I was asleep when I felt the tarpaulin being dragged off. Some man had come out of the building and was trying to get past me. He must have been a cook or a cleaner just finishing his shift and on his way home.

'You can't sleep here.'

'Sorry.'

He could tell by my voice I was a woman. He seemed surprised and bent down to take a closer look. I was still half asleep and disorientated, and I looked back into his bearded face in the sinister dimness.

'You're a girl!'

I didn't answer, just got to my feet and started to move

away, dragging the tarpaulin with me. He followed, and I was getting ready to run.

'Wait!'

I turned.

'We could go inside, where it's warm. I could get you something to eat.'

'You a good Samaritan, then?'

'I'm sure you can think of some way to repay me.'

I threw the wet tarpaulin at him and ran out of the alley. I was into the street and scampering like a delinquent child and I could still hear his shouts coming after me.

'Whore! Slag! Lesbian!'

It was about 3.00 a.m. and I decided to stay out on the brighter busier streets and forget the dark alleys. I found a porchway into a bank and tried to rest there, but I was moved on by the night security, who kicked and gruff-voiced me away. I was afraid I'd be picked up by the police and have to spend the night in the cells – and that might have been the safest option, but they might also have tried to get in touch with my family and I couldn't risk that. The morning light came slowly, creeping up over the flat landscape to the east. I only managed to snatch small pieces of sleep during the long night, sometimes only minutes, before attracting the attention of some shifty opportunist idiot and having to move on. I was glad when morning came and I sat in an early coffee shop and warmed my hands round the cup. I stayed there until I got conspicuous by my presence, then decided to patrol the Coventry Road to see if I could 'earn' enough money for a room. If I got lucky, I'd check in to one of the cheap hotels or bed and breakfast places on the Hagley Road and crash out for the rest of the day.

I was getting a bit nervous on the Coventry Road. I'd walked it a lot and it was getting too claustrophobic, too familiar, mocking at me. I was worried that, sooner or later, someone would recognize me. But I had no choice right now, I didn't want to spend another night in the doorways. I was looking a bit bedraggled after my night on the streets and didn't know if I'd be able to connect with anyone. Then a shiny new Mercedes pulled up along-side me. A young Asian man rolled down the window. He was thin as a coat hanger and I didn't recognize him – it seemed safe enough. He smiled.

'Where you going, girl?'

'Nowhere. I got nowhere to go.'

He opened the door and beckoned for me to get in. I hesitated at first, because I had a bad feeling about this, but I put it down to nerves-on-edge from being out on the street and, anyway, I really had no choice. I didn't real-ize there was another man in the back until I was in the car and the driver locked the doors. I glanced at the other man's face in the rear-view mirror. I knew him. He was the young Asian I'd conned on my very first streetwalk – the one driving the BMW, who I'd left in the fast-food shop in Small Heath. He looked at my reflection before speaking.

'So, you're homeless, then?'

'That's right.'

'Lot of homeless girls on the streets these days.'

'I suppose so.'

I was trying to stay cool, but I was really sick with fear. My heart was beating like a nervous drum and I was sure they could hear it. The one in the driver's seat turned to the other one.

'This her?'

The man in the back seat leaned forward, grabbed my face and turned my head round. He looked at me closely.

'How much a cheap hotel room?'

'I don't know.'

'You don't know?'

'I stay in a hostel.'

He pushed my face away from him with a look of disgust in his eyes. Then he lit a spliff, took a few drags out of it and passed it to the driver. I immediately knew it wasn't weed – Alice was always smoking weed and I knew what it smelled like. This was something different and it seemed to get them instantly excited – agitated. The driver handed the spliff back to the guy in the back seat.

'Well?'

'Nah, it's not her. She was special, man, not a scrubba like this one.'

The driver unlocked the doors and I jumped out of the car. It roared away up the Coventry Road and I wasn't sure if the man in the back seat really didn't recognize me or if he just didn't want to admit to his mate that he was deceived by such a draggletail as me.

But it was a close call and I knew I couldn't chance the streetwalking and conning any more. I might not be so lucky next time – next time it might be the guy who abducted me. I'd be too nervous from now on and I'd give the game away before I even got in someone's car. I had

enough money for another cup of coffee and ten cigarettes to steady my nerves, and then I went up to Broad
Street, trying to think what I was going to do. I decided to
go back to the refuge and it was getting dark when I finally
arrived there. But they said I'd been gone for more than
three days and I'd broken the rules, just like Alice did, and
now someone else was sleeping in my safe bed. The support worker had her I-told-you-so face on and said I
should go to the hostel on Sand Pits they'd given Alice as
an alternative. It was better than the streets but it was a
distance away and, by the time I got there, it was closed
for the night.

I was still on the streets with nowhere to go.

I walked through the city centre, trying to stay in the
bright lights, but keeping my hood up and my face hidden. Drunks kept coming up to me and putting their arms
round me and I patted them down, searching for their
wallets. But I wasn't very good at pickpocketing and they
thought I was getting fresh with them and tried to kiss me
and slip their hands between my legs, and I had to break
away from their beery breath and sly eyes.

And there were still eight more nights to go before I
got my flat.

It was getting very late. The streets were emptying of
the evening people and the night people were emerging
for their nocturnal prowls. Pimps and pushers and dregs
and dropouts – but I was one of them now, wasn't I? So
what did I have to be so proud about? I'd fallen as low as
I could go and I was part of the underbelly of society –
unseen by respectability – visible only to those of the
same faecal colour. I hung about the better-lit streets for

as long as I could with my hand out, hoping some man would take pity on me and give me money. But I no longer looked all glittery and glamorous. I looked like I'd been dragged through a hedge backwards and no one wanted to know. I was just another beggar, another down-and-out in a city full of such fools. The power of physical attraction had evaporated and now I had no assets left. No weapons to work with.

I needed to sleep. I was out on my feet from being awake all through the night before. I made my way along to the subways under the Five Ways roundabout. They were littered with big cardboard boxes. I didn't know if people were inside them or not and I was afraid to look. Finally, I found one that was open and empty and I moved it away from its location to another subway – in case its owner came back and found me sleeping in his bed. Like Goldilocks. It was uncomfortable on the hard ground, even with the cardboard and my coat underneath me. I was nervous in case I got attacked and I closed the box up, with a piece of clothing sticking out so creepers and crawlers could tell there was someone inside, but couldn't tell if it was a man or a woman. I was hoping they wouldn't want to take the chance to find out.

It was that time of early morning when it isn't quite light, but not bible black either. I woke with a start to the feeling there was something in the box with me – something moving around. I was too petrified to move, in case it was a rat or some other such animal that would attack me if I stirred. I tried to accustom my eyes to what little illumination there was from a distant street lamp – to expand my irises like a cat. I had the strap of my bag wrapped round my wrist and now I felt something tugging at it, very gently at first, then a little stronger. When the bag didn't give, whatever it was let go and everything was still and quiet for a moment. I remained motionless, hoping if I just lay there it would go away. Then something touched my face – it was bald and warm and it had fingers. It was a hand!

I screamed and emerged from the cardboard box at the speed of light, still clutching my bag with one hand and lashing out with the other. I was confronted by a boy of about twelve or thirteen, who was more startled than I was and turned to run away. I don't know why, but I called after him.

'Wait!'

He stopped running. I approached him slowly. He backed away.

'I won't hurt you.'

He stopped backing away when he realized, by the sound of my voice, that I was a woman.

'What were you looking for?'

'Money.'

'D'you think I'd be here if I had money?'

He didn't answer. He was short, smaller than me, with dark hair and rough, dirty skin. He wore a short-sleeved T-shirt and lightweight trousers and trainers, and I thought he must be cold in the pre-dawn chill. He could have been a gypsy, I wasn't sure.

'What's your name?'

'Tommy. What's yours?'

'Tammy.'

He laughed.

His teeth were good, but stained, and I could tell they hadn't seen a toothbrush for some time. His hair, though short, was matted and his nails were long and dirty underneath. But he had an endearing and innocent smile that belied his sense of street wisdom.

'Tammy and Tommy.'

I laughed with him. He came close and looked me up and down and told me it was dangerous for me to be sleeping here. I could be raped or beaten up or even killed. I told him I had nowhere else to go and he mulled the situation over in his mind.

'Stick with me.'

It was just getting light when I followed him through the subway complex and out into the street-level air. He shivered a bit and I took a cardigan from my bag and draped it over his shoulders.

'Haven't you got a coat?'

'Yeah, but I can run faster without it.'

As we walked, he told me he came down to the subways sometimes to see what he could steal from the hobos and the homeless, and sometimes there would be drunks collapsed and drug addicts out of their heads. It was a dangerous occupation; he carried a couple of scars where he'd been cut and his young nose was broken from a hard fist he'd taken full in the face. I asked him why he did it – the pickings couldn't be very rich in a place like this.

'Better than in town. No police at night.'

And he was right. Nobody cared who robbed these people – they could be attacked by drunken youths coming from the pubs, or robbed of their few possessions by rascals like Tommy, or set on fire by psychopaths – nobody cared. There would be no recriminations. No punishment or price to pay.

I followed Tommy out away from the Five Ways roundabout and along the waking Broad Street for a short distance. Then we took to the alleys and backstreets and I was wondering if I should trust this boy I barely knew. He could be taking me anywhere – leading me into some kind of trap.

'Where we going?'

'Somewhere safe.'

That's all he said. I kept following, across the canal and along Holloway Head and past the Hippodrome and the Bull Ring. We finally arrived in an area of Digbeth I hadn't seen before. It was under the Duddeston Viaduct and was a maze of derelict industrial buildings and warehouses. A network of rubble-strewn streets spider-webbed their way through the area and collided at an intersection of river, canal, railway and ring road. It was a jumble of decay and crumbling brickwork and empty meat-market spaces and fragmented factories – all being slowly reclaimed by nettles and weeds.

As we made our way through the desolation, I could see signs of life beginning to stir amongst the makeshift shelters of tarpaulin and corrugated tin and cardboard and plastic sheeting. It was a forlorn and desolate place. Dirty faces were repeatedly illuminated in the weak light by flashes of fire, as crack pipes were lit for the first fix of the day. Tommy must have seen my expression of apprehension and he told me not to be afraid.

'How many people are here?'

'Dunno, maybe a hundred.'

He said no one knew how many for sure, they came and went, or died, or got taken into hospitals or homes or refuges or police stations. The pungent stink of crack cocaine drifted on the breeze like burning plastic. For those who don't know, crack is a comparatively cheap drug with a short-lasting high, so the addicts are always on the edge, waiting for their next 'hit'.

We kept moving through the desolation, both structural and human, until we came to a large, red-brick building on the edge of it all. Tommy pointed towards the door and handed me my cardigan back.

'Aren't you coming in?'

'Not yet.'

'You should be in school.'

'That's where I'm going.'

I knew it was a lie. He knew I knew and he laughed. I looked away, towards the building, and when I looked back, he was gone.

I went inside and found that part of the place was occupied by a local charitable group that provided a drop-in centre for alcoholics. I told them I wasn't an alcoholic but I was homeless and on the streets. I was getting a one-bedroom flat in a week and I just needed a place to stay until then. A member of their resettlement team saw me and said he could contact a women's refuge for me – it was the one I'd left with Alice and I knew they'd just refer me back to the Dickensian hostel on Sand Pits again. So I was going round in circles. But I didn't tell him I'd been thrown out for breaking the rules.

'I know where the refuge is. I'll go round there.'

'You're welcome to stay for breakfast. We serve from 9.00 a.m. to 10.00 a.m.'

So I did. Then I picked up my bag and hit the streets again.

One week to go.

9
Survival

I made my way back to the hostel on Sand Pits, before it got too late to get in there. It was a dive of a place, but better than the other options I had – which were none. They didn't have any spare beds, but they had a dormitory that I could use and they gave me a second-hand sleeping bag until a bed became available. It was smelly and sweaty and stale, but it was better than nothing and at least I'd have a roof over my head and a place to wash and brush my teeth. The hostel closed its doors earlier than the refuge, at 7.00 p.m. That was to stop the crackheads outside from coming in and interfering with the women. After that, there was only one member of staff on duty for the night and it was like bedlam inside. There were about forty women of all ages crowded in there and half of them were drunk or high on drugs. Some were right rough-looking sorts and I decided to keep the lowest profile possible. I could have had a shower, but I didn't dare risk leaving my bag alone because I knew it would be gone when I came out. So I washed my hair and body in a hand basin and brushed my teeth and lay on top of the sleeping bag for the night.

Apart from the rooms, the dormitory itself was over-crowded, with about twenty women wedged in there, while there was really only room for about ten. Alcohol wasn't supposed to be allowed on the premises, but a group of the older women had smuggled in some cheap vodka in water bottles. This was the stuff that turns your eyes yellow and they were getting really aggressive with each other. The one staff member on duty was too scared to intervene and, eventually, at about midnight, the inevitable fight started. In a crowded space like the dormitory, once something like that kicked off, everybody got sucked in. Bottles and bags with house-bricks in them and stiletto shoes and chair legs were used, and blood and broken glass was showering everywhere.

I quickly jumped off the sleeping bag and got my back up against a wall. Like I said, my dad had taught me how to fight and I defended myself and my bag of possessions in the mad mayhem of the dormitory. Girls were screaming and trying to get out, but the doors were locked and full-scale panic set in. Other women were coming out of the rooms and joining in. The staff member was hysterical and crying, and didn't know what to do, until someone screamed at her to call the police. Which she did. By the time the police came, there were bodies all over the floor and those who could still stand were trying to escape. A big blonde woman staggered my way, her hair in a frenzy all over her face and her fists clenched.

'I know you.'

'No you don't.'

'You're the one who –'

I hit her in the throat before she could finish accusing me of whatever it was she was going to say I did. Some of her friends saw what happened and came at me, while the blonde woman clutched her neck and made choking sounds. Three of them half circled, but couldn't get behind me because of the wall. They were all older and heavier than me and I braced myself, waiting for them to make their move. But, before they could headbutt me or grab my hair, the doors opened and the police came swarming in. Those who were closest to the now-open doors made their getaway out on to the street, but I wasn't so lucky. I was arrested and handcuffed and thrown into the back of a waiting paddy wagon.

At Birmingham South police station, they took my shoes and my belt, and locked me in a cell for the night. The place was overflowing from the hostel fight and they put another girl in the cell with me. Her name was Monica, or so she said, and she was young and crying. She'd never seen the inside of a police station before – or so she also said. But I had, plenty of times, with my nan, and the place didn't intimidate me at all. In fact, I was glad to get away from the bedlam of the crazy hostel and get some peace and quiet for a change – if only I could get Monica to stop crying.

'You're safe in here.'

'I'm sorry, it just freaked me out.'

'Relax, try and get some sleep.'

There was only one bunk in the cell and no blankets, but it was warm enough and we lay down together and she stopped sobbing.

'Have you got anything?'

'Like what, Monica?'

'Something to calm me down.'

'Are you kidding? This is a police station. I was searched at the desk . . . Weren't you?'

'Yes, I was . . . But I just thought . . .'

That I was a criminal type and might have something concealed in one of the orifices of my body. She could see I was angry and apologized, then started to tell me her story, how she came to be in the hostel. She was from a good home, but her brother had been sexually assaulting her from a young age. Her parents believed the brother and the abuse continued until she couldn't take it any longer. She'd run away a year ago, when she was sixteen, and had been in and out of a variety of institutions since then.

And I thought, you don't really get a feel for what life is like at the bottom of the hill until you roll down there and live with the people who've slipped and can't get back up on their feet again. How many women were there in the world like Monica and Alice and Zena, and all the others I'd met since I'd left the artificial womb of London? How much abuse was going on? The general public didn't know the slightest thing about this subculture, this undercurrent of damaged women that flowed beneath the facade of society. They didn't know about the river of pain and suffering that washed up against their safe closed doors in the night and then receded into the shadows when the camouflage of the civilized morning came. And it made me feel so frustrated.

The police threw us out without charge the next day. Monica and I made our way back to the hostel to retrieve our bits of belongings, which got left behind in the mêlée of the night before. It was about 10.00 a.m. when we turned the corner, and there on the street outside the door talking to some crackheads were the women who'd attacked me – all four of them, including blondie. I stopped dead in my tracks. Monica looked puzzled.

'What's wrong?'

'Nothing, you go on.'

'What is it, Maggie?'

Maggie was the latest name I was using. It was clear I couldn't go back to that hostel, unless I wanted to have my nose repositioned to the back of my head. But I had to get my bag. Everything I had in the world was in there.

'I need you to get my bag for me, Monica.'

'Why, where you going?'

'Anywhere except here.'

I told her to just go in and find the bag and, if anyone asked, to say I'd been kept in the police station and I needed my identification.

'All right.'

'Good girl.'

'As long as I can come with you.'

No, not again! I'd already done this for Alice and I didn't want to make the same mistake twice, even if Monica didn't have a child in tow. It was hard enough to look after myself on the streets and I knew she'd be a liability. But she wouldn't go get my bag unless I agreed.

'OK.'

I still had six nights to go until I got my flat and there was no way I could do it without my bag and my meagre belongings.

Once she got our stuff out of the hostel, Monica and I headed back into the city centre. We sat begging on Broad Street for a few hours and made enough money to buy some food and a packet of cigarettes. And, while we were eating, Monica told me the rest of her story. Her brother had given her heroin and she'd taken it in order to endure his abuse, but now she was an addict and on a methadone programme. She got the methadone fix at a clinic near Brookfields Cemetery every day. She had to go over there for 2.30 p.m. and I went with her. Afterwards, we hung around the area and begged a bit more, but didn't manage to make much money from the locals. We slept in the cemetery that night, huddled together behind a big head-stone and covered over with our coats. We thought we'd be safe there as most people would be afraid to go into a graveyard at night because of the ghouls and ghosts and poltergeists and pink elephants.

It must have been about 1.00 a.m. when we heard weird noises coming from the other side of the tombstone. We were really frightened at first, then we craned our necks to look over the stone to see what was happening. It was only some young lad and his girl getting down to it – hugging and snogging. An owl hooted at the same time as Monica and I peered over the headstone. The girl looked up to see two pale and haggard faces looking down at her. She screamed and nearly scared her boyfriend back into his trousers. The two of them grabbed their clothes and took off running as fast as they could. We found a packet of cigarettes and a half bottle of vodka that they'd left behind, and we laughed and Monica had a drink, even though she shouldn't with the methadone – and I had an unexpected cigarette.

Next morning, I had my social security money, which was £80, and only five more nights till I got my flat. Monica and I spent some of the money on food and essentials, then we went down to Mosely Road Baths and bought two tickets for the pool. We swam in our underwear because we had no swimsuits and attracted a few raised eyebrows, then we showered and put on some make-up in the changing rooms. I paid for a twin room in a cheap hotel on Hagley Road and that left us with £20 between us. So we headed for the bright lights of the city centre. I felt clean and almost back to my old self again, and I wanted to dance and forget the days and nights on the squalid streets. We chatted the doormen into letting us into a club for free and we stayed on the dance floor, letting go of everything and losing ourselves in the music. At least I did.

Monica, just like Alice, was on the prowl for marijuana to ease the addiction pains of the heroin that even the methadone couldn't completely eradicate. After a while, I missed her from the dance floor. Then I saw her over by the bar, talking and laughing with a couple of men. I was about to go across to make sure she was all right when I recognized the men as two of the group from the ladies' toilet – the ones that made the cut-throat and bullet-in-the-brain signs at me as I got that other girl away in the taxi. What could I do? If they saw me I'd be in big trouble and this time I didn't have enough money left to escape them in a cab. But I couldn't leave Monica there with them, to be gang-banged in an alley somewhere – or worse.

It soon became obvious to me that Monica was telling the two men she was with someone and I was out dancing, because they started looking my way. I dodged behind a pillar, but they started walking towards the dance floor and it was only a matter of moments before they'd see me. So I grabbed my coat and made for the exit. On the way out, I gave the doormen a description of Monica and the two guys she was with and asked them to watch out for her because I believed she was in danger. They looked at me like I was some kind of lunatic, but it was all I could do. I waited in the shadows across the street from the nightclub for a while, but I was attracting the attentions of drunken droolers passing by and I knew if they came out of the club they'd see me.

I went back to the hotel in Hagley Road and waited.

I hardly slept that night, waiting for Monica, but she never turned up. I had to be out by 10.00 a.m. next morning, so I left her bag at reception and told them she'd be coming for it. I had no money, so I couldn't book the room for another night. But I had to try to find out what happened to Monica, so I went to the hostel and hung around until I was sure blondie and her mates weren't there, then I went in and asked if she'd come back at all. They didn't know any Monica, so I knew it wasn't her real name. I looked round, but couldn't find her, and I couldn't stay in case the tough women showed up with their crackhead friends. I had to get £40 from somewhere so I could go back to the hotel and wait for Monica. If she didn't turn up that night, I was going to go to the police. Streetwalking was out of the question, I was no good at pickpocketing and begging wouldn't get me enough. There was only one thing for it – I had to steal something that was valuable enough to sell and make me the money. Jewellery would be too risky and clothes too bulky. It would have to be something electrical and small. The

Don't I look angelic? This is me, aged four, when I lived at 49 Crutchley Road in south east London with my nan.

Me and Dad in happier times. Not long after this photograph was taken, my dad went on the run and my mum walked out in the middle of the night.

Goofing around with Uncle John, when I was five. Apart from my nan, I was always surrounded by men when I was growing up.

At Santa's grotto, aka a supermarket in Lewisham! Despite my upbringing, I was really just a normal, well-behaved kid who loved school.

This was my eighth birthday. You wouldn't know it by looking at me, but by this age I had already seen so much.

Here I am, aged nineteen, when I was working at the bank. As my family became reliant on my income, I started to spiral into debt and depression.

Fast forward a few years – there aren't many photos of me during the lowest time of my life. This is my daughter, Alyssia, who turned everything around for me.

Celebrating Alyssia's birthday at Drayton Manor. I remember being determined to hide my fear about my cancer surgery the next day.

A selfie taken at our new home in Thirlmere Drive, Birmingham! Moving here made me feel happy and safe for the first time in years.

Reunited at long last with my nan after my family got in touch to tell me that they missed me.

My nan, Eileen Mackenney, at a signing for her book, *Borstal Girl*.

Alyssia and I in our home in Birmingham a few years ago. I couldn't face going back to London so Eileen came to live with me and Alyssia.

All the girls together! Nan, Alyssia and me.

Xbox had just come out and it was a big boy's toy. I knew I'd have no trouble flogging it in one of the pubs. The expensive electrical goods would all have security tags, but I'd been brought up in a house full of criminals and I knew all the tricks of the trade.

The first thing I had to establish was my escape route. So I chose a shop that was out of the way, but close enough to a busy thoroughfare with lots of exits off it, so I could get lost in the crowd if anyone came after me. Next, I'd have to be quick. A woman like me carrying a bag would arouse suspicion as soon as I walked in, so I had to know exactly what I was going for and where it was located. Normally that would be established on a previous visit to the shop, but there wasn't enough time now. I waited somewhere inconspicuous until a teenager came out.

'Do they sell the Xbox in there?'

'Yeah.'

'I'm not sure what it looks like. Where are they located?'

'Halfway down on the left.'

'Thanks.'

I waited again, until a smartly dressed man walked into the shop and I walked in right behind him, linking his arm like I was his wife or girlfriend. He looked surprised for a moment, until I let go and went straight to the Xboxes. I picked one up and made like I was going to the counter, but instead I walked straight out of the door. The security tag set an alarm off immediately, but the shop staff were confused and started asking the man if I was with him. By the time he convinced them I wasn't, I was out on to the main street, weaving through the crowd, then ducked down an alley on the other side and disappeared. I made my roundabout way back up to Broad Street, carefully keeping an eye out for patrolling police, in case they'd caught me on CCTV.

I went into a pub that looked like the clientele might have a spare £40 to pay for a knocked-off Xbox. There were a couple of guys at the bar who seemed like the sort who played computer games.

'Anyone want to buy an Xbox?'

'No thank you.'

'It's brand new.'

'How do we know?'

'Still got the security tag on it.'

I gave them a look and they liked what they saw, but it would depend on the price.

'How much?'

'A hundred.'

'Give you forty.'

'Sixty.'

'Fifty.'

'Done!'

I walked out of there and went straight back to the hotel in Hagley Road to wait again for Monica.

I had four nights left to go before I could get the keys to my new flat.

It was about 4.00 p.m. when I got there and her bag had already been picked up. I asked the receptionist and she said a young woman had come for it. I asked how she looked and was told she looked tired. I was relieved. I booked the room for another night and hoped she might come back. But she didn't. And I never saw her again. But that's how it was with missing people, they appeared like phantoms out of the mist of their misery for a few moments, then they disappeared again. They might reappear for a brief period somewhere else – or they might not. No one could really know.

Next morning I left the hotel at 10.00 again. I had £10 left and three days to go till I got my flat. I was nervous about hanging around the city centre in case I'd been caught on CCTV, so I kept out of the way that day and slept at the back of some houses in Lightwoods Park. The night was uneventful and nobody disturbed me except a few dog walkers who gave me a wide berth.

Two nights to go.

On the second-last day, I decided to go back out to the refuge to see if they'd let me back in for forty-eight hours, but they wouldn't. I met one of the girls I knew outside who said she was going to a party that night and I could tag along if I liked. It would probably be a late one and at least I'd be in somewhere. So I went. The party was wild and carried on all night and I didn't get much sleep because I was trying to fend off a flurry of male testosterone – at least, the men who couldn't make it with anyone else and thought a tramp like me would be easy as eating ice cream. I only snatched a couple of hours in the early morning when they were all wasted and I hung around as long as I could the next day and took some food and a bottle of water with me when I left. I had only one more night to survive until I was safe inside my own little hideaway, away from the raw edge of this rotten world.

When it began to get dark, I went round to Noel Road where my new flat was located. It was one of those big Victorian houses that had been converted and my flat was on the top floor. I slipped in through the security entrance when someone came out and I slept on the wooden boards of the stairwell and waited outside the door for the housing officer to come with the key the next day. Which he did. Then I was inside and safe. I'd hung on to what was left of my morals by a single thread. I'd done things that I'd despised and frowned upon all my life and I was a hypocrite and I hated myself.

But I'd survived!

10

The Flat

When I first went into the women's refuge, it was explained to me that this would only be a temporary measure and I had to fill out an application for housing with Birmingham City Council. The support workers attached a letter confirming that I was living at the refuge and was, in effect, homeless. The application went to the council's homeless team to be assessed and I was told the process normally took six to twelve weeks. The application asked which areas of Birmingham I'd prefer to be housed in but, as I didn't know the city, the support workers picked for me. After the twelve weeks were up and I hadn't been offered anywhere, I rang the council. They said there were no properties available in my chosen areas, but they had a few properties in Edgbaston if I was interested. I wanted a place of my own as soon as possible, so I said yes.

Thank you.

Noel Road was a small suburban street that ran off Monument Road, a larger thoroughfare. What I didn't know was, to get into the city centre from Noel Road, I'd have to turn into Monument Road and then walk down the Plough and Harrow Road. This was a notorious red-light area of Birmingham and that's why the council had flats available in the vicinity. But nobody thought of telling me at the time and I just wanted somewhere to live.

The flat was empty as a broken heart when I first moved in. But an empty flat was better than a park bench or a subway tunnel or a bus station in the dark shadows. The electric meter wasn't working properly and I couldn't see my hand in front of my face on that first night. It was the beginning of October and cold as well, and I had to sleep on the bare floorboards. I'd applied for a grant to help me furnish the place, but they turned me down because I didn't have any children. They did give me a crisis loan of £200, which I only got on the evening I moved in, because that's how the application process worked. But I was just happy to have somewhere to live and I believed in my heart it would only be a matter of time before I got everything I needed for a narrow and abnormal little life.

Next day, I went out and bought pillows and a duvet, and some plates and pots and pans. I put money in the electric meter, but something was seriously wrong with it and it still wouldn't work. I had to wait for an engineer to come out to fix it and that could take ages. I went round the second-hand stores to see if I could get some cheap furniture, but there was nothing I could afford.

Because I was still suffering from the euphoric effects of the post-traumatic stress disorder, none of this really registered with me. It didn't matter that I was cold and aching when I woke in the morning, or that I had no food and couldn't afford to heat the flat, even after the meter was fixed, or that I bathed in cold water and hand-washed my clothes and was becoming emaciated and strange-looking. Or that I got ill with bronchitis and couldn't breathe properly and had to be put on inhalers. It didn't matter because there was a locked door between me and the menacing world outside.

When I wanted there to be.

I had no money to do anything and I couldn't just lie on the floor, cold and hungry all the time. So, after a few days, I decided to go out on the scrounge again. There was still no electricity in the flat, so I had to stand outside on the freezing cold landing and use the security light to get changed and do my make-up. Then I went out and walked along the Plough and Harrow Road for the first time. It was night and the journey took me into a surreal world that I'd never seen before, even when I was on the streets. Cars started to kerb crawl along beside me and, when I looked around, I could see there were women standing on the pavements like they were waiting for something. The cars were pulling up and they were getting in, and then the penny dropped. They were prostitutes – and the men in the cars thought I was a prostitute too! The women looked grotesque – wrecked – like painted zombies, and I didn't want them thinking I was one of them and was trying to move in on their territory. They gave me dirty looks. Some were really rough and some were pitiful and some were menacing and some had a hardness in their eyes and others looked at me in a pleading kind of way. One, who was close to me, looked about fifty, with no shoes and matted hair. She was as thin as a stick and may have been on hard drugs of some kind because there was no life in her eyes. Another one was disabled. There was something wrong with her knee, it looked twisted and deformed, and she couldn't walk properly. A car pulled up down the road and she tried to run to it, stumbling along and in through its opening door. It was sickening – stomach-churning. It was so distressing it almost made me cry. As bad as my situation was, these poor women were worse off than me. But I never cried and I couldn't then. Even though I wanted to.

I quickened my step as shady-looking men moved close to me in the sinister street-dark, with their leering mouths and their evil eyes, and tried to rub themselves up against me. Cars were parked up and down both sides of the road and, as I passed, the doors swung open and hoarse voices came from inside.

'Are you busy?'

'Are you working?'

I started to run and didn't stop until I was into Hagley Road.

When I lived in London, I witnessed a lot of crime and violence, but I never saw a single prostitute. When I was at the refuge with the massage parlour next door, I knew what they were up to inside, but it was out of sight, not up close and in my face. I wasn't all that scared and it was usually daytime and the refuge was close by. During the whole time I was abducted, I was either drugged or high on adrenaline, so I didn't have a chance to be really afraid. And even when I was streetwalking and conning, the men I met weren't out looking for prostitutes, they were young and just trying to get lucky, and I wasn't going to give anything out – it was like a game. This was different – dark and nasty, filthy and dangerous. I felt weak and vulnerable, and I didn't like it.

Once I got to Broad Street and all the bars and clubs

and fast-food places, I was feeling really hungry – I couldn't remember the last time I'd eaten. I stood outside a burger bar and pretended to be crying. It wasn't long before some drunken man came up and asked me what was wrong. I told him my pocket had been picked and I was hungry and couldn't afford food. So he gave me a five-pound note. I found that when older men were drunk, most of them were quite generous, especially to a younger woman. The power of physical attraction again – I'd lost it for a while but, now that I had a place to live, I was determined to get it back again. Maybe not to the same extent as before, but enough to get me by. And I wondered what the difference was between what I was doing and what the women in the Plough and Harrow Road were doing – was there any difference? I told myself I was just trying to survive. And so were they! But it seemed different to me. What I was doing was temporary, just till I got on my feet, and I wasn't giving anyone sex. Now I had my flat, I'd get it furnished eventually and get a nice job and become a mouldable member of accepted society again. It was just a matter of time.

On the way back, I tried to avoid the Plough and Harrow Road by going across a high-rise estate. There was a large green area with a park and swings in the middle, with tower blocks on either side. I wasn't sure if it was any safer than the road, but I had to get home some way. A couple of teenagers came up, driving a boy-racer type car and, as I tried to turn into the grassy area to get across to Noel Road, they pulled up beside me and asked if I wanted a ride. I ignored them and walked straight on, and this obviously annoyed them because they began revving the car up. It jolted to a halt directly in front of me and they started calling me names.

'Slag!'

'Hoor!'

As I turned to walk away across the park, they mounted the kerb and drove across the grass after me. There was no one else around and I started to run. I saw a light up ahead, coming from a little community centre place, and I hoped there was someone in there. I ran through the door and found a cleaning woman, just ready to close up and go home. I explained what had happened and she let me stay for a half hour until I thought they'd gone. I was very cautious when I came out and hurried the short distance to my flat. I decided to stick to the streets after that – even if it meant passing the prostitutes.

I saw those boys again later, coming out of a local off-licence – they didn't even recognize me.

I thought I'd be really happy once I got my own flat, but there was an emptiness in me that was reflected in the bareness around me. The absence of anything in the space I occupied. I don't mean furniture or carpets or curtains: there was no emotion – it was an empty shell with no personality and no comfort and no love. And I was its living personification, bare and empty. I had no direction, no function, no purpose. Nothing. So I went up to Broad Street every night to see if I could find what was missing. But all I found was the lonely silence that surrounded me in the midst of the meaningless noise.

Eventually, the electricity got fixed and Alice's mother

got fed up with her – or Alice got fed up with her mother – and she and Emily came to live with me, like I promised they could. She brought with her the sound of her dejection and the odour of her disappointment, and they permeated the flat and filled up its emptiness. I'd told Alice I had no furniture and she asked her mother to help. The woman brought down two second-hand beds and a fridge and television. But we didn't have any tables or chairs and we had to use boxes as substitutes. As soon as Alice came, it was like she'd never been away and we were back in the refuge, only with more freedom and no sense of responsibility. She'd leave Emily with one of the girls we knew from the refuge, who had three children and who'd got housed close by, and life was a mixture of clubbing and partying practically every night, in a vain attempt to keep the demons of our respective pasts at bay.

Alice had been offered a place of her own as well, a two-bedroom house in Winson Green, close to the prison. We went out there to see it and the first thing we noticed was the filthy streets, strewn with rubbish and beer cans and all sorts of excrement. It was one of those squashed little terraced houses that stepped right on to the pavement outside. When you're homeless, you're at the very bottom of the council's list and they can offer you a place where nobody else wants to live, and you can't turn it down. If you do, you're taken off the homeless register and kicked to the kerb. Most of the houses in the street were boarded up and only one or two were occupied. It seemed like the place should have been demolished back in the damp and dreary olden days. We didn't have the keys and we were trying to look through the windows to see what it was like inside. The neighbour next door poked his head out.

'What are you ladies doing?'

He said it in a sickly sweet way and he looked to me like he might be a child molester. Alice answered him.

'I've been offered the house and I wanted to have a look at it.'

'You can come in and have a look at mine.'

Again, the oily double entendre. We went in and he was giving us the once over, looking us up and down. I expected him to tell us how bad it was around here but, instead, he said how much he loved the area and how Alice should get herself a cat when she moved in because there were a lot of rats about. I think he really fancied having Alice as a neighbour and I didn't like the way he was looking at Emily.

Alice turned the house down and the council kicked her off the homeless list. And that's why she came to live with me at Noel Road.

We'd both go down to Broad Street, the 'drinking mile' of Birmingham, to get some coarse and garish colour into our grey little lives. And every time we did, I bumped into the muscle man who I'd told I didn't fancy that day and he'd start shouting at me all over again – calling me a slag and a whore and a lesbian. He was always hanging around the area and I got fed up with this harassment every time I went into town. So one day I just went up to him and called him away from his mates. He was grinning back at them, as if to say 'I've sorted this bitch out, boys.'

'I've got a photographer friend.'

'That so. He take pictures of you naked?'

'No, but he takes pictures of kids' birthday parties.'

'So?'

'I got a couple of pictures of you on my mobile.'

That was a lie, I didn't even have a mobile, but he didn't know it.

'If you don't leave me alone, I'll get my mate to super-impose your face on a naked body and place it with the kids at one of those parties, then plaster it all over this city.'

He never bothered me after that. In fact, whenever he saw me coming, he ducked down a side street or into a pub.

Alice and I would go into the clubs to meet up with some of the other refuge girls we knew and I'd hit the dance floor. The power of physical attraction came back and we used men to get what we wanted – money and drinks and food and, in Alice's case, marijuana. It's not something I'm particularly proud of now and it was only all right with me to begin with, but I knew deep down it wasn't how I wanted to live my life. I'd started to think I had some mental health issues I needed to sort out and eventually I felt myself growing apart from the other girls. I didn't like this life. I wasn't totally depressed or anything, but I wasn't happy either. Sometimes I'd come home in the early hours, carrying my shoes, and I'd climb out through the skylight window on to the roof. There was a little ledge and I'd lie on it and look up at the stars. It was quiet up there and I was all alone, and I felt so small in the big blustering world. It was the only place I'd allow myself to think about my past, my family, everything that had happened – and I permitted myself to wonder how every-one was, if they still lived in Nan's house or if they'd lost it by now. Because of me. Would they ever forgive me? What if I'd done things differently?

Where was I going?

What was I becoming?

I was having a lot of trouble at the flat since Alice moved in. The novelty of the clubbing and parties was wearing off for me, but not for her. She'd bring men back without telling me, and her boyfriends were all drinkers or drug-takers, and some of them were violent. She was always having fights, because she could be as aggressive as any of them and would never back down. Sometimes I thought she actually wanted them to hit her. It seemed to me she related to violence and abuse in some strange way and she welcomed it like an old lover. She'd push them to the limit and they'd be ready to walk away – but she wouldn't stop, calling them names and throwing things until they hit her and I'd have to jump in and risk getting hit myself.

One particular time she was arguing on the phone with this guy she was seeing on a regular basis. I knew it was getting dangerous because he was making all sorts of threats and she was shouting back at him.

'Come on then, come over and get me!'

Then she dropped the phone like it was on fire and stood back looking at it with a shocked expression on her face.

'He's coming to get me, Shelley.'

I didn't know what to do. Except that we should certainly get out of there until he cooled down. Then I heard a banging on the security door downstairs and it sounded like it was getting knocked off its hinges. Someone must have opened it because then there was a stamping up the wooden stairs. I grabbed Emily and the three of us bolted out the back way and down the fire escape and out through the alley at the side of the flats.

We ran up the street to the grassy space between the tower blocks and we hid in the park with the swings for a long shiver-shaking time, until we saw his car drive away up the road. When we got back to the flat, the door had been kicked in and the place was trashed. It was bad enough before because I never had much money to buy stuff, but now it looked like someone had come in with a sledgehammer and destroyed what little was there. The beds and television were smashed and the skylight was broken and stuff had been thrown out through it into the back garden. It took me ages to repair and replace everything, and we had to sleep with no door because the housing association refused to give me a new one, so we had to wait until I could afford to have it replaced myself. And Alice was back with him within a week. She wanted him to come round to see her, but I said no! She told him this and he threatened to break my jaw. When I went out, she brought him round anyway.

Another night, we'd been to a club along Ladywood Middleway and we were on our way home. We went a roundabout way along Alston Street to avoid the Plough and Harrow Road, and Alice decided she wanted to bring some beer back. There was nowhere open except for what looked like a working men's club. When we went inside, it was full of Rastafarian types. I mean, it was wall to wall with black men – and no women. There was hardly any room to move. We were both wearing tight minidresses and everything stopped when we walked in – the music, the conversation, everything! I grabbed Alice's arm and tried to get her to come back out, but she insisted on pushing her way through to the bar. When we got there, they wouldn't serve her and she started shouting abuse. I dragged her away and tried to get us back out through the throng, but there were too many bodies blocking the way. I felt like a kitten that had accidentally fallen into a yard full of pit bulls. Then I noticed a side door and made a move that way, dragging Alice after me. The whole place stank of weed and I was nearly choking by the time I got back out into the air. The door led to an alley and there was a gate leading out to the street – but it was locked. We had to take off our shoes and hitch up our skirts and climb over the gate to get out. Just in time. We ran the rest of the way back to the flat – and she didn't even get her beer.

I eventually got a job doing evening shifts in a supermarket and I used to get home late at night, sometimes in the early hours. Every time I did, Alice would be there with men I didn't know, getting smashed. I'd be wet through from the rain or freezing from the cold and they'd be there, laughing and drinking and smoking weed in my flat, and it began to really annoy me. It was coming into winter and I had to do a late shift one night and Alice had arranged to go out. I asked her to drop the keys in to me at work. It was 2.00 a.m. when I finished and no keys had been left for me. I walked home, but couldn't get into the flats. I spent an hour trying to get through the main security door, but no one would open it and it was snowing and

I was only wearing my light supermarket uniform. I finally got through the front door, I can't remember how – either someone buzzed it or I opened it by pushing and rocking it. But I couldn't get into my flat and Alice wasn't answering her mobile. I had to sleep in the stairwell again, just like I did when I was homeless. By the time Alice got back the next day, I felt the cold had penetrated my bones and I thought I might be suffering from hypothermia. I put on layers of clothes and got into bed, but couldn't get warm no matter how I tried. I'd never been that cold before in my life – it felt like even my eyes and nails and hair were frozen and I was thawing from the inside out.

And that's what Alice was like – she would be so kind and considerate when she was sober, but when she drank and took drugs, it was all about her needs and nothing for me and Emily. I considered asking her to leave many times – many times. But then I'd look at little Emily and I just couldn't do that to her – not after all we'd been through. And I conditioned myself to believe that I deserved this life. Normal people didn't live like this, but I didn't think of myself as normal. We were all messed up together. I didn't feel a part of proper society and I had no right to complain.

But Alice kept on pushing my patience to the limit. She'd chat to men in the street, just to get weed, and when she got it she'd invite them back to the flat and I'd come home from work and there'd be men and marijuana everywhere. I didn't want this any more. I was trying my best to set down some kind of foundation for my life. I had a job and was earning money and I couldn't go out every night like before because I had to work. And, anyway, I didn't want to. The party girl persona didn't suit me. It was all right for a while, but now it was time to try and get my life back on track. I'd had a breakdown and fallen apart and everything I'd been through was part of the recovery process. Now I was trying to regain my stability – trying to put myself back together.

Humpty-dumpty.

Alice didn't like this and she felt I was no longer the friend she'd known. And I probably wasn't. We started arguing all the time and I wondered how long we could go on like this. I asked her to register as homeless again, because she'd be eligible to go back on the list after six months. I really wanted her to get a place of her own and I was worried that the housing association would find out she was living with me and kick us all out and then we'd be homeless again. Back to the streets and parks and behind the bins and inside the cardboard boxes.

It was getting to the point that people she'd chatted to in the street were turning up at the flats uninvited, and pressing the buzzer and shouting outside, and I couldn't get any peace or quiet or privacy. I even broke the buzzer in my flat, thinking if I didn't answer they'd go away. But they only buzzed the other flats and that made matters worse. I was getting threats from people she owed money to and the situation was becoming intolerable. I began to understand why her mother couldn't cope with her and maybe everything wasn't all that woman's fault. Maybe Alice's disillusionment with life was too much for her to bear and she couldn't watch while her daughter destroyed herself. Nobody knows the full story of why a person acts the way they do, except that person themselves. I tried not to judge Alice by my own dubious standards, but I suppose the old adage isn't too far from the truth.

Familiarity was breeding contempt.

Thinking back now, I would hate to have had to go through all that with my daughter Alyssia. I couldn't have done it and let her see what little Emily saw. I'm always very careful about the impressions I give her because, ultimately, I want to teach her to be more than just a woman: I want to teach her to be a lady and to have respect for herself.

11
Working Girls

After the incident in the high-rise park area, I was nervous about crossing it again at night, so most of the time I had to walk along the Plough and Harrow Road to get home to the flat. One night, on my way back from working in the supermarket, I was walking fast with my hood up and my head down, so as not to attract the attention of any of the men or the working women either and trying to get to Noel Road as quickly as possible. Suddenly I heard a searing scream and I looked up to see a big man punching one of the prostitutes on the other side of the street. He hit her again and she screamed again. I was going to walk on and just ignore the incident, but it didn't look like he was going to let up. I slowed down and waited for someone to intervene, but nobody did. Everybody shied away and hid their heads behind their trepidation. He hit her again and she fell to the ground. He was about to kick her, as she curled herself up in foetal fashion.

'I've called the police!'

The sound of my own voice surprised me – it was hoarse and fearful. I didn't have a mobile phone, so I waved my compact case in the air, hoping he wouldn't be able to see it clearly in the dim street light. He stopped threatening the woman and started to cross the road towards me. I didn't know what to do – if I ran he'd surely catch me and he was too big and burly to try and fight. As if by providence, a police siren sounded a few streets away. The brute glared at me with menace in his eyes for a moment and I could smell the misogyny coming from his heart. Then he turned and ran off.

I went across to the woman. She was bruised and bleeding, and I helped her back to her feet. She was in her mid thirties, with black hair and heavy make-up and she was wearing a miniskirt and a red plastic coat.

'Thanks, luv.'

'Are you all right?'

'I'll be fine.'

She looked at me closely.

'You're new.'

'I'm not a . . . working girl.'

'No?'

'No. I just live nearby.'

She didn't look fine to me and I advised her to go to the hospital and get checked for broken bones. But she wouldn't hear of it. She said she lived in Monument Road, not far away, and asked if I'd walk with her because she felt a bit dizzy. I didn't want to get involved, I had enough problems of my own, but I felt sorry for her and I was worried in case she got weak and fell over – or the thug came back to beat her again.

'Who was that man?'

'A punter.'

'Why was he hitting you?'

She said he wanted her to lower her price and, when she wouldn't, he got angry. She told him to go to one of the older prostitutes – they were cheaper. But he wanted her for some reason and he kept getting angrier and angrier. When she tried to walk away, he hit her.

'Occupational hazard, luv.'

She shared a flat with two other prostitutes and she invited me in for a drink as a way of saying thank you.

'Oh no, I better get home.'

'Look at you, you're shaking, luv. Come on, you need a cup of strong sweet tea.'

Noel Road wasn't far away, but she was right, I *was* shaking after the confrontation with the lout, even though I hadn't noticed until she said it. Maybe a cup of tea would steady my nerves. But I still hesitated, as I didn't know who might be inside the flat. She seemed to know what I was thinking.

'There's no one home, you'll be all right.'

She told me her name was Holly and she was twenty-six, even though she looked much older. Her face was the face of an older woman and her eyes had lost their sparkle – if they ever had any sparkle. The flat was clean and tidy and had two beds in one room and one bed in another. It had a sitting room and a small kitchen and a bathroom and looked comfortable enough – certainly better than my flat in Noel Road.

'I've only got vodka.'

'You said a cup of strong tea.'

'I was joking.'

'Tea is good. I don't drink much.'

'If that's what you want.'

She made a pot of tea and poured me a cup. I put three spoons of sugar in to see if I could calm down a bit and stop my headstrong heart from beating furiously. Holly cleaned herself up and poured a large neat vodka. She looked very pale without her heavy make-up and I was still worried in case she had some internal injuries and might pass out.

'When will your flatmates get home?'

'Could be any time. Who knows?'

'You want me to wait until they do?'

'Would you?'

I could see she was a bit perplexed that someone who was just passing by would stop and help a prostitute like her. I didn't tell her I was a missing person or that I'd been homeless or anything else about my life. But she started to talk about hers.

She was born in Liverpool and was abused by her father when she was young. He was a violent man and he beat her mother when she tried to intervene. The mother was afraid to complain to the police or to leave him, because she said he'd find her and kill her. Holly ran away from home when she was sixteen and spent some time on the streets in Liverpool. I found myself unwillingly empathizing with this young woman, after my own harrowing experiences, but I kept my business to myself. Holly was 'recruited' by a pimp in Liverpool and went on the game as one of his 'string'. He introduced her to heroin and crack cocaine to keep her working for him. He took most of the money she earned in return for a place to live and a regular supply of drink and drugs. But he was as violent as her father and she had to get away from him before he killed her – and she had to get far enough away so he wouldn't be able to find her. She went to Nottingham first and from there down to Birmingham, where she'd been working for a couple of years now.

'It won't be safe for you on the Plough and Harrow Road now, Holly.'

'It'll be all right.'

'What about that guy? What if he comes back?'

'I'll hide if I see him coming.'

'You should report him to the police.'

'You're not serious?'

She laughed drily and it hurt her face. She took a big drink of the vodka to ease the pain, emptying the glass. Then she filled it again.

'Sure you won't have one . . . what's your name?'

I cast round in my mind for a name I hadn't used before – then I remembered the girl from the hostel on Sand Pits.

'Monica. I'm OK with the tea, thanks.'

'Not Lewinski?'

She laughed again and hurt her face again and drank again, obviously not believing my off-the-cuff alias. I was curious and asked her why she continued to work in this dirty and dangerous profession.

'It pays better than minimum-wage shop work, luv.'

She told me she didn't have a pimp now, she was free-lance and could keep all the money she made. But that had its drawbacks too.

'If I had a pimp, that guy wouldn't have got away with hitting me.'

'You should get a pepper spray.'

'Bad for business.'

'Why?'

'Word would get round. If the guys knew I was packing pepper, none of them would come near me.'

Just then, the door opened and another girl came into the flat. She was about the same age as Holly and dressed in a silver coat and silver boots and a cheap silver lamé minidress. She gave me a suspicious look before turning to Holly.

'Holly, what happened?'

'Some guy got physical.'

'Are you OK?'

'Thanks to Monica Lewinski here, she frightened him away. This is Silver, Monica.'

'Of course it is.'

Silver was instantly wary of me. She looked me up and down and went behind me and looked at me from the back, then came round and stared straight into my face.

'She a copper?'

'No, I'm not.'

'Lesbian?'

'No!'

'What are you then, a good Samaritan?'

'If you like.'

She sneered, cynical that any such thing even existed.

She took off her silver coat and poured herself a vodka, and she and Holly compared notes about the night's business. I was feeling calmer now, so I stood up to leave.

'Don't go, Monica.'

'You'll be all right, now Silver's here.'

'Have another cup of tea.'

It was just a friendly invitation, and I realized these

women were ordinary people like everyone else, who had experienced extraordinary things in their lives. Maybe their plight was their own fault and maybe it wasn't, but who was qualified to sit and judge? Certainly not me! I poured another cup of tea from the pot. They tried to get me to drink some vodka, but I wouldn't. It wasn't that I wanted to be prudish or that I was totally against alcohol, but it was a strange place and, even though I felt relaxed, I didn't know these women and I wanted to keep my wits about me. Silver took out a crack pipe and gave me a look that said it was her house and she didn't care if I approved or not. They both tooted on it while they drank the vodka. I was in no hurry to get back to the flat in case Alice had some boisterous house guests. So I stayed.

'Don't you bring the punters back here?'

'No. Against the rules.'

'Whose rules?'

'Madam's.'

I didn't ask who Madam was. I presumed it was the other woman they shared the flat with.

The booze and crack relaxed Silver and she wasn't so wary of me after a while. I guessed she was probably already high before she came in, or maybe on the way down after a hit and needed another. She was a single parent, but social services had taken her two children away from her because they were undernourished and neglected. This upset me a bit because I hated hearing about kids being misused and not looked after properly. But I tried not to form a biased opinion and dislike the woman – I didn't know what she'd been through in her life. Like Holly, she seemed to know what was going through my mind.

'You want to know why my kids were neglected?'

'I didn't say anything . . .'

'Not that it's any of your business, Monica Lewinski, but I'm an alcoholic and I drank all the housekeeping money.'

To give her her due, she was frank and honest about it. But her tone was hostile and unapologetic.

'You're right, it's none of my business. I don't need to –'

'I'm ashamed of it, if you really want to know.'

I didn't really, but she kept talking. After they took her kids away, she drank all the rent money and, with no children, she was thrown out on to the street.

'That's when I met Madam.'

Silver said her goal was to get off the game as soon as she could and find a proper job and get her children back. I couldn't see how she was going to do that, considering she was sat there swilling vodka and smoking crack cocaine. She saw my scepticism.

'You don't believe me, do you, Monica Lewinski?'

'Like you said, it's none of my business.'

'Well, for your information, I'm going into rehab as soon as I get a place of my own.'

It was impossible for her to quit drinking and smoking in a flat with two other prostitutes who both drank and smoked heavily. But she was saving her money and would soon be able to rent a place by herself. She wanted to move away from the Plough and Harrow Road and had her eye on a little maisonette over in Edgbaston. Then she'd go into rehab and, when she came out clean, she'd get a good paying job. She said she was educated and could work as a secretary or a personal assistant or something like that. When social services saw how well she was doing, they'd have no option but to let her have her children back. I was still sceptical, but tried not to look it. At least her intentions were optimistic, even if they were unachievable, and I thought maybe I should start believing like that myself.

'Either that or marry a millionaire.'

They both laughed loudly at this, like it was a private joke between them.

The door opened again and an older woman came in. She was about forty, but could have been older under her heavy make-up. She looked at Holly first.

'Not again!'

Then at me.

'Who are you?'

'She's Monica. She helped me.'

The woman was dressed in a faux-fur coat, with a red dress that was too tight for her and fishnets and very high heels. I could tell she was wearing a wig and false eyelashes and I wondered what else about her body was duplicitous. She kept looking at me suspiciously.

'Are you social services?'

'No, I'm just –'

Silver answered for me – sarcastically.

'A good Samaritan.'

The older woman took off her coat.

'I don't trust good Samaritans.'

She poured herself a vodka and Holly filled her in on how I'd helped her get rid of the abusive punter.

'Very brave of you.'

'Or stupid.'

'Leave Monica alone. She's my friend.'

I wasn't her friend — nor did I particularly want to be. But there was a spirit of camaraderie in the flat, despite Silver's sharpness, and it was like we were all women and could understand each other. I still didn't talk about myself, even though they asked me a few questions. And they didn't really want to know, which suited me.

The older woman was the Madam they were talking about earlier. It was her flat and the other two paid her rent. She joined in the conversation after a drink and I found out she was once a high-class hooker who plied her trade in the posh hotels and top-end brothels of London and Paris and Amsterdam. She claimed to speak several languages and had lived in Italy and Sweden and Germany when she was younger. But they were the golden days. Now she couldn't compete with the younger girls and was considering coming off the streets altogether and going into the telephone sex business, or 'dial a wank' as she called it. It was much safer, but the money wasn't as good. I didn't really want to know but she explained you just had to be a good actor, that's all. They were called adult chat lines and were run by service bureaus.

'Like call centres?'

All three of them laughed at my naivety.

'Not exactly. You use your own phone and your own home.'

No good to me, I didn't have a phone or a home. She said, in a rather refined accent, that she'd advertise in the men's and pornographic magazines and the customers would pay her by credit card. But she'd be independent, because the bureaus could take half her earnings. She'd

even set up her own Internet website, listing her specialities and services. We laughed together about what those
specialities might be and she said you could be whoever
you wanted to be on the end of a phone line where no
one could see you. She was a wickedly witty woman and it
was probably her elegant audacity that had got her through
her colourful life so far.

I asked her how she ended up on the Plough and Harrow Road, after being the toast of all the big cities in
Europe, and she told me she married a man from Solihull
who lied to her about being a millionaire. That made the
other two giggle again – but not too overtly. He'd said he
was a high-class hotelier, but he only owned a backstreet
pub and he had her working behind the bar and washing
glasses and mopping the floor and cleaning the toilets. So
she left him, but not before she took enough money from
the till to put a deposit on this flat.

The vodka bottle was empty and Holly was half asleep
by the time I left. Dawn was breaking out on Monument
Road and all the hookers and their punters had melted
away like vampires, as if the rays of the morning sun
might burn them to ashes. The whole place was deserted
and I was able to stroll safely home in the peaceful earli-
ness. Alice and Emily were both asleep when I got in, so I
went straight to bed. It was a strange experience, being
with the working women, but they were just people like
everyone else. They'd been dealt a bad hand in life's game
of cards and they were playing with what they had, trying
to survive in their own way – maybe the only way they
knew how.

I saw Holly once or twice more on the Plough and

Harrow Road and she always waved to me when I was passing. Then she disappeared and I never saw her again after that. I never saw Silver or Madam again either, and I wondered if Silver really did go into rehab and if Madam went into the phone-sex business and was specializing with all the lonely deviants out there in the sex wilderness.

12
Pregnancy

Alice came back one day after leaving Emily for a while with her mother and said she was going out that night with a man she had been seeing. His cousin was coming with them and she asked if I fancied making up a foursome. I was feeling a bit down at the time, a bit morose – melancholy – trying to either cope with Alice or ask her to leave, and not knowing how I was going to do either. So I thought why not, if you can't beat them, join them. And it might cheer me up and give me something to think about other than myself and my martyrdom.

When we met I knew I'd seen this man before, but I couldn't think when. He had beautiful eyes. We ended up in a pub, which wasn't ideal for me, but he was very pleasant and charming and funny and I liked him.

'We have met before, you know.'

I pretended not to know, in case it was at some time or in some place I didn't want to remember.

'Have we?'

'Yes. You were wearing a very sexy catsuit.'

Then it came back to me. He was the man who'd asked me if I was all right that day Alice went off and left me with Emily, and I'd marched into the pub after her. I'd pushed him out of the way and he'd nearly fallen over.

'Was that you?'

'Yes.'

His name was Marco. He was Italian and laughed with his eyes, and I laughed with my mouth, and we really hit it off after that and I ended up spending the night with him.

Next day, I was disappointed with myself for having given in so easily and I didn't intend to see him again. But I did. I kept bumping into him and, gradually, we ended up together, like it was fate. I wouldn't say I loved him, but I liked him and he liked me. I'm not impressed by macho or muscles or ego or arrogance or aggression. I grew up with all that and Marco was never that way. He made me laugh and that worked for me. It was a thing, we were lovers, and my feelings for him grew. I felt a kind of attachment to him. I didn't go sleeping around like some of the girls, so when I found someone I liked, I stuck with him. He became a significant part of my life at a time when I needed something significant to sink into – something to surround the bareness of my existence and pad it out. Give it an essence.

But, when I look back now, he wasn't a good choice.

Marco was a self-employed courier, doing multi-drop deliveries all over Birmingham and Solihull, and he asked me to be his navigator. He'd pick me up and I'd plan the quickest routes and give him directions, and we'd laugh and talk about everything in the cab of his van. I came to know all the different areas of Birmingham and I'd spend all day with him driving around the countryside and singing to the radio. I allowed myself to believe that I could be happy. Marco drank a lot and smoked marijuana but, in the beginning, I didn't realize the extent of his habits. Whenever I went out with him, we'd go to pubs or clubs and we'd be surrounded by booze, and he held it very well. The more he drank, the funnier he became. You have to understand that every single person I knew was drinking and taking drugs. To this day, I've never seen so many drugs – I was surrounded by the culture. So, Marco's drinking didn't seem excessive at the time.

But then one night we had a party at the flat in Noel Road. When I woke next morning, there were glasses everywhere, half full of all kinds of spirits – vodka, whisky, gin, brandy, liqueurs, beer and other stuff as well. I was about to empty them into the sink when he came in, poured it all into a pint glass and drank it down. It was only 6.30 a.m. It made me wince.

When I was growing up, I never ever thought that I'd have children. As long as I can remember, I always thought I wouldn't make a good mother. I think it stemmed from the fact that I believed my own mother wasn't a good mother, at least not to me, so how could I be a good mother? Her badness would have seeped into me in the womb and I was afraid I'd become her. I never had much interaction with babies or young children. When I moved in with Nan I was in a house full of adults and never had younger children around me. At school I was very much a loner and when I went to work in the bank I didn't even consider having a child, because I loved my work so much. I would see some of the staff getting pregnant and leaving, and they'd come back to show off their babies and everyone would go 'ooohh' and 'aaaahh', but I never got that broody feeling and I couldn't see the appeal. I think I'd mentally blocked that part of me off because I was afraid I'd do it all wrong, like I did everything else wrong, and somehow hurt the child, just like I'd been hurt. So, I was convinced I'd never, ever have a child of my own.

Then a strange thing happened. I started having a recurring dream – that I was pregnant. It might have been normal for any other woman, but not for me. I'd wrecked everything I'd touched in London and now I was paying the price for it. So why was I having these dreams? I never wanted to get fat and go through labour. Nappies and baby sick and crying all night were alien to me – anathema. I was too selfish to put up with all that. Oh, I liked kids, as long as they were somebody else's and I could give them back. But I couldn't shake the feelings I was getting. I started looking at women with their children and wondering what it would be like to have a child of my own. Then I looked at Alice and Emily, and I thought, no – I wasn't in a position to give a baby a good chance in life with all the craziness that was going on in the flat. I knew this, but the thought of having my own little child just wouldn't go away. It buzzed round me like a persistent bee.

I dreamed of a little girl with dark curly hair and big brown eyes in a red dress. It was so vivid and we were so good together and I'd wake up happy. Not like the happy you get when you buy something new or have a drink or sex or something – not happiness that wears off. The feeling made me believe the world was a wonderful place. I didn't know what it was, I certainly hadn't found what I was looking for when I left London. Freedom didn't do it or friendship or anything else. I couldn't get back what I'd had when I'd been working at the bank and that was a sense of pride and belief in myself. I really didn't know what it was, but it was what I wanted.

The thing I had with Marco was always going to end. I knew he really wasn't the man for me – but he was the best one I'd met in my sorry life so far. I needed something to really love, something that would love me in return, something permanent in my elusive life – a reason to keep on living and planning for the future and trying to be a proper person. It took me a while to come to terms with it, but I finally decided I needed to have a baby. People will say that's the last thing I needed in my chaotic life – why bring a baby into that? But they'd be wrong. The more I thought about it, the more it seemed so right to me. I didn't take the decision lightly. It wasn't an accident like it is with so many girls. I really questioned what it would be like to have a child and I worried if I could be a good mother. I knew I wouldn't be like the women I'd known who left their kids with anyone so they could go drinking, or left their babies outside pubs or with people who wouldn't look after them. But then, my mother had left me and I didn't want to do that to my child.

In the end, the pros outweighed the cons.

So I went ahead with it.

I didn't trick Marco – I told him. I told him I wanted a baby. I told him I was coming off the pill and I wanted to get pregnant and become a mother. I had to tell him because I wanted him to have a choice about it. If he'd said no, I wouldn't have done it, but I'd probably have found someone else. I wasn't out to trap anyone and I didn't even need him to be a father if he didn't want to. He told me he'd love to have a baby with me. He told me he loved me and he'd be proud to have me as the mother of his child.

I fell pregnant in late autumn. I was working at the time and I remember missing a period and feeling permanently hungry, which was unlike me. I took a pregnancy test and it was positive. I screamed with delight and anyone would've thought I'd won the lottery. It was what I'd wanted and now it was going to come true. In a single moment, the whole outlook and purpose of my life changed. I was going to be a mother. I had a little life inside me and I would love it and love it and love it for ever. I knew it would be a girl because of the dreams I was having and I knew I'd call her Alyssia, which meant 'enchanting'. But when I told Marco, he was less than enchanted. His expression said everything. I knew he hadn't taken me seriously when we spoke about having the baby and, now it'd happened, he didn't want it. He smiled and tried to act pleased, but his smile didn't reach his eyes.

Things became different between us from then on. He didn't make me laugh any more and I didn't make his eyes smile. The supermarket promoted me from the late shift to the checkouts and he would come in and get a bottle of vodka and a packet of mints. He'd pay for the mints and expect me not to scan the vodka, and he'd walk out with it. What could I do – have him arrested by security? He was the father of my unborn baby. I told myself I should, but I just couldn't do it. He got away with it a few times but then I started scanning the vodka and he had to pay. He didn't come back into the shop after that.

I got to thinking though, if I could do it for Marco,

I could do it for people who really needed it. This woman came to my checkout with a small entourage of children and I could see she didn't have much. She was trying to add up the price of each item she was putting on the conveyor, to see if she could afford it. I started deliberately not scanning some of the items, the more expensive ones like meat and nappies and baby food. I saw her looking at the till total and she realized what I was doing, but she said nothing. She bagged up the stuff as quickly as she could and her eyes said 'thank you' to me before she hurried out of the shop. I kept doing it – if a mother came to my checkout and she looked like she hadn't enough to feed her children, I wouldn't scan some of the stuff and she'd be so grateful, even though she wouldn't say anything. Word soon got round and people kept coming back; everyone would queue for my checkout rather than go to another one.

But that wasn't why I got caught. I used to wear a really short skirt in the supermarket and what I didn't know was that the security camera was 'following my legs', as they put it. One day I was letting a poor woman through without scanning all her stuff and she was stopped on the way out. I knew I'd been rumbled, so I went to the café and smoked a cigarette while I waited for them to come for me. And they did. They called the police after having a laugh and telling me about the CCTV following my legs, and I was taken away and spent the night in Steelhouse Lane police station. The police treated me like I was some notorious criminal and I wondered if they knew about my family. I'd changed my name, but they still had my real identity from the time I first came to Birmingham and gave it to Missing People and asked them to get in touch with my family to let them know I was all right. I was worried they might contact my father or my uncles again and tell them they had me in the cells. While I was locked up, the police raided my flat and searched it inside and out for stolen goods and went through my belongings and cross-examined me about fraud, just because I had Alice's bank card in my bag. They were really nasty to me – so they must have made some connection.

I went to court the next day and was given police bail until my case came up.

I lost my job at the supermarket and was taken back to court a month later. I pleaded guilty because I just wanted to get it over with and I asked my solicitor to explain that I'd had a nervous breakdown and was suffering with post-traumatic stress disorder. The magistrates were unimpressed by my psychological problems. They gave me a lecture about how giving away food to the poor warranted a custodial sentence but, as it was my first offence, they gave me five hundred hours' community service and fined me £200 instead. I really needed some kind of counselling or therapy, but the court didn't see it that way. The magistrates decided that, if it wasn't prison, I had to make significant reparation to the society I'd offended. But because I said I suffered from depression, I was told I could do some mural painting and that was the only concession they were prepared to make to my undiagnosed mental health issues. I love art and all things creative and I had an A* in art from school, so I believed I'd landed on my feet and I smiled politely back at the stern faces behind the bench.

I was sent to see a probation officer in Selly Oak and it was arranged I should do the community service in a place down the road from the probation office where they were painting murals for schools and churches. It was miles from the flat and I had to walk all the way to a big kind of shed at the back of a bail hostel. Inside, there were a dozen or so benches and stools, and we had to stay there all day. It was freezing in the place and there was no heating and no toilets and no facilities for food of any kind. The teacher was pedantic to the point of being supercilious and, instead of being artistic, like I thought it would be, it was brain-numbing and soulless. I was made to mix the paint and clean the containers, and it was only after six weeks of this drudgery that I was allowed to actually paint something. They were working on a huge mural for a church and I was allowed to paint the brown bark on a tree. I didn't complain, as it was meant to be a punishment and not a privilege, and I went regularly every week until my pregnancy advanced and I didn't want to walk that distance any more. I couldn't stand the cold either and I was suffering from morning sickness and my bronchitis was being affected. So I went to the doctor, got myself signed off sick and the community service was put on hold.

After the community service ended temporarily, I went out to the cinema with Alice one evening – I'd completely stopped going to pubs and parties and doing any kind of dangerous or dodgy stuff since I'd found out I was pregnant. I was very protective of this little life I had growing inside me and was adamant I wasn't going to put myself or it in any jeopardy. I was a few months gone and beginning to show a bit. It was about 10.00 p.m. when we came out and some man she knew asked her if we wanted a lift. I said no.

'C'mon, Shelley, it'll be OK. I know him.'

It was a mistake, of course – I could feel it in the pit of my stomach, but I got into his car. It was only a two-door so, once I was in, I couldn't get back out. Alice was in the front, chatting away to this man, and I was in the back. At first I told myself I was being neurotic and it was just a lift home. But he kept on driving all the way to Coventry and wouldn't stop to let me out.

'Let me out of this car!'

'Keep your wig on, I just gotta pick something up from my mate.'

'Yeah, calm down, Shelley. It's OK.'

I tried to be calm, for the baby's sake, but I remembered the abduction and being in the back of that fast-moving car and I just wanted to be at home where it was safe. He didn't pick something up at his mate's – he picked his mates up instead, and their girlfriends. Four carloads ended up driving to an underground rave thing in Coventry. Once there, I found the darkest, quietest corner of that place, hoping no idiot would bother me. Alice went off with the man and his mates and their girlfriends to get smashed. It was a free-for-all. I'd never seen so much white powder in my life. They were snorting it openly off the tables. I got a bottle of water and held on to it for dear life, in case some clever dick tried to spike it like before and I ended up in that state again. I was so afraid something would happen to my child. I was sitting there for five hours and, from where I was, I could see how messed up the girls were getting as the night wore on. Strangely enough, the men didn't seem nearly as smashed as the women.

One of those girls had been telling me on the way there about her little sons and how much she loved them and how beautiful they were. By the end of the night she was lying on the floor twitching and making weird noises with her mouth, and I thought she must be hallucinating or having a fit of some kind. She started to vomit and it was all in her hair and she couldn't get off the floor. She was trying to get up on all fours to steady herself, but she kept slipping back into the vomit. The man who was with her walked away and left her. I had to leave too. I didn't want to, I wanted to get her some help, but I didn't know where or how. I was in a strange place with no money and no mobile phone, and the only means of transport was about to walk out the door. I couldn't take the chances I took before. I couldn't get myself involved in danger like before. I had to be responsible now and look after myself and my baby.

So I left.

I didn't speak the whole way back. I just wanted to get away from them as quickly as I could. As soon as we got to Birmingham, I got out of the car and walked the rest of the way. I felt so sick and needed the fresh air. It was a turning point for me. I knew I didn't want this kind of life for my daughter, I wanted something better for her. So the next day I started to put plans in place to get myself and my life sorted out. I would not be like that girl left on the floor.

I would be with my daughter and give her everything she needed in life.

I was really getting sick and tired of all the things that were going on at Noel Road and I started to think that, even if it was what I deserved, it certainly wasn't what my unborn child deserved. I had to find a way out and into a proper life. I learned that a high street insurance company was advertising for customer service assistants and I really liked the look of that job. It was just what I needed, working in an office with products I had experience of selling. A good, solid, professional job that I could really get into. I filled out an application and was invited for interview. I performed well at the interview and assessments and was accepted for six weeks of in-house training. For the first time since leaving London, I felt I'd found something that would make up for the loss of my job at the bank. I wanted to get that back and join the mainstream of society again.

I went to the Jobcentre and signed off the benefits I was getting. I hated taking social security. I felt I was better than that and I liked working; I *wanted* to work. I gave them details of the insurance company and when I was starting, and I walked out of there with my head up. I had some money left from my job at the supermarket, so I went out and bought sensible clothes from a local charity shop and I started to look like a dignified woman again. One of the things I bought was a long white duffle coat. I always wore red lipstick and my hair was black, so they started calling me 'Snow White' at the insurance offices. I liked the people and I seemed to fit in. I felt respect for myself coming back along with the confidence and professionalism I'd lost when I left the bank. I understood the products I was handling and I enjoyed the office atmosphere. The people were different too. They liked to go for a night out but they knew when it was over. They weren't excessive and they didn't do drugs. They went home after a few drinks and got up in the morning for work. I could relate to them and I liked the feeling of normality. But that feeling left me every time I went back to the flat and the empty life encroached again.

The insurance building itself was in the town centre and it was part of the redevelopment I'd seen on that first morning when I stepped out of the Bull's Head and walked up the hill. It had everything an employee could want: canteen and gym and free Internet access during break times and an amicable ambience of smiles and simple cohesion. I'd arrive early to get away from the flat, go up to the top floor and look out through the big glass windows at the world rushing by below me. And I felt so good. My mentor and trainer at the office was also a life coach and I spoke to her about everything. She was quite religious and very sincere, and I felt comfortable confiding in her. Our conversations were never awkward – never intrusive. She really helped explain what options were open to me and where I should be going and how I could make choices, and she was starting to change the way I looked at life and the way I focused on the future.

After the training, I was allowed to choose which department I thought would be best for me – sales, claims, recoveries or customer services. I chose recoveries, which meant taking on a claim and liaising with the other side to recover funds due. It might seem a bit dry, but I'd worked in sales before and didn't relish cold-calling again. I preferred taking something on from the start and bringing it to its conclusion. It gave me a sense of satisfaction – like I'd actually achieved something.

Everything was going great and the spiritual sun was shining again, until one morning I came into work and the manager called me into his office. He said my family had been on the phone, trying to find out where I was.

'What did you tell them?'

'Nothing. I said I could tell them nothing.'

I couldn't understand how they'd found out I was there. It turned out they knew someone working in social services in London and they'd been trying to track me that way for some time. It was all right while I was in the refuge because it was a safe house and only had a PO box address. Once I moved to the flat, that was a different matter. But I also changed Jobcentres and it took the London informer some time to trace where I was now signing on. Then I got the job in the supermarket and the trail went cold, but I got sacked and had to go back to the Jobcentre. Then the informer found out about the insurance company. And, if they could do that, they could find out where I was living. I knew I had to leave, because it was only a matter of time before they came up here and were waiting outside the door for me some evening. I wasn't ready to face my past and I had to vanish again. I resigned from my job and went back to the Jobcentre, where I made a formal complaint to the authorities, backed by support staff. This was a very serious matter and I said the leak must have come from Catford social security office. The manager there was contacted and told to warn his staff that any more leaks would result in sackings and prosecution. The trail went cold again.

But I couldn't count on it staying that way. I had to get out of Noel Road and I had to get an official name change, not just another alias. Shortly after, I changed my name by deed poll. I went to a solicitor in town and his fees were paid by legal aid. He drew up a formal name change deed, showing my old name and my new name. I signed it and it was legally binding. I registered on the electoral role in the new name and used a different date of birth.

I was no longer Shelley Mackenney.

I wasn't happy at having to leave the job, but I'd had to walk to work and back during the first month until I got my pay cheque and I couldn't afford to eat or heat the flat either and I was really feeling the effects of the cold. It all took its toll on the pregnancy. I was exhausted and light-headed and sick in my stomach. It felt like I had weights pulling me down, dragging me down to the ground. Then I started to pass out. I'd be OK one min-ute, then I'd feel all funny like the room was moving and the world was spinning inside my brain and I'd just faint. I also felt like my stomach was turning over and I was bleeding slightly. I was sure something was wrong and I was petrified I'd lose the baby. So I went to see the doctor. I told her everything. It all gushed out of me like a tidal wave of panic and I asked if I could be losing my baby because of my life and the badness in me. She sat listening patiently and didn't look at me as if I was completely crazy. She did some tests and discovered I had a kidney infection and that was the reason I felt so bad.

She also encouraged me to have counselling for my mental health condition.

'When, doctor?'

'Immediately, I think.'

I'd always known I needed some sort of counselling, but now it was finally being offered to me, I was nervous and didn't want the stigma of having mental health issues on my medical record.

'Why, doctor?'

'You need to come to terms with your life before your baby is born. Otherwise it may manifest itself as postnatal depression.'

I wanted to be a good mother and if that meant counselling, that's what I was going to do.

So I went to a session once a week for an hour at a time. It was located in a small office at the back of the doctor's surgery. The counsellor was a middle-aged woman and she sat there knitting while I talked. It was relaxed, there was no set agenda, and the woman looked like someone you would sit next to at a bus stop, not a clinical psychiatrist in a white coat.

She listened and I talked. I talked and talked and talked and talked – about how I was feeling and what my fears were at first. Then I talked about my past and my family and my mother. I talked about falling apart and not knowing what to do any more or where I belonged. Over time, all the feelings I had been suppressing started coming out, in a controlled way and at my own pace. It was like my mind was a crowded elevator and every time the doors opened, stuff spilled out. I told her I was afraid I wouldn't be able to love my child, that she'd be born and I wouldn't be able to cope and she'd be a stranger to me. I was destined to fail in everything I did in life and this would be no different. All the memories came back – all the failings and hurt and guilt and anger and despair and resentment and bewilderment and loneliness and the big gaping hole inside me that had turned to ice.

The counsellor didn't take these feelings away from me. She didn't wave some magic wand and make them vanish. All these things were buried under the surface and I needed to bring them out so I would understand how they were affecting my life and the choices I made. She got me to realize why I'd made mistakes and why I had compulsions like the shopping addiction and why I could never say no to people like Alice. The counselling helped me understand what I was feeling deep inside me and, when those feelings manifested themselves in everyday life, I could recognize what they were and start to take control again. While I was hiding from everything, I was really hiding from myself and fooling myself into thinking that everything would just go away if I ignored it. If I didn't confront the reasons why I was here in the first place, then I'd just end up making the same mistakes all over again. And I'd be like Sisyphus, pushing his stone up an endless hill.

And I had to admit – to myself – where I went wrong, where I could have done things differently, so that if I found myself in a similar situation again, I wouldn't go down the same road. And I had to forgive myself for my mistakes. That was huge. I'd had guilt issues all my life, for being born and for my mother leaving and for being a burden to Nan and for deserting everyone the way I did.

The guilt didn't go away with the counselling, but I learned to let go of the past because it couldn't be changed and to look to the future with a different point of view. I kept going to counselling for about nine months – all through my pregnancy and right up to when my daughter was born. I never missed a single session. I felt renewed after each one – cleansed. I realized my family were only human and I let go of all the anger I felt about getting into debt and admitted the part I'd played in that, as well as everybody else. But I still wasn't ready to go back. I was going through an emotional exploration of myself and it wasn't over. I was trying to repair myself and I didn't want anything to interfere with that restoration work. At least, not until it was finished.

The counsellor told me about people she'd met who were damaged and who'd moved on and overcome their difficulties – people I could relate to – so I didn't feel I was a freak or unique. The feelings were normal and I needed to have them, but I could control them and not allow them to control me. I realized I wanted to be loved. I realized I wanted to be wanted – to be worth something – to prove I was worth something.

I realized that I was human after all.

13
The Unit

What with the leak of information to my family and all the things that were going on in my flat with Alice and her freaky friends while I was out working, I had to get out of there and find somewhere else. Now, because I was pregnant, I had to give up work altogether and I was back there all the time in that unhealthy, volatile atmosphere. But the counselling had given me a new sense of direction. I realized that everything must change in a changing universe – and my consciousness was dealing with that changing detail, not the universal constant of existence. I was determined to get myself out of there and to find somewhere safe and peaceful and conducive to the later months leading up to the birth of my child. I simply refused to bring my daughter into that kind of life. She deserved better and I was going to give her something better, because the sum of myself now was becoming greater than the haphazard months and years of who I was before.

I took Alice to the housing office to see if I could get her re-registered as homeless – I couldn't trust her to do it for herself because she'd probably have met someone on the way and gone drinking with them. But she wasn't eligible, as she was classed as becoming intentionally homeless by getting herself kicked out of the refuge and refusing the house she was offered in Winson Green. I then contacted the refuge and asked if I could go back there and be re-homed and Alice could keep my flat for her and Emily. But they were having none of it. I told them I was pregnant and unable to cope and I feared for the safety of my baby if I had to stay there. After a lot of begging and pleading, they told me about a new mother and baby unit that was opening in a few weeks' time and that there would be ten places available. But there was already a lengthy list of girls applying and it would be a long shot. They gave me a number which I called and said I wanted to apply for the specialist housing at the new unit. They also told me there was a long list of people to be assessed and I needed to be aware that places were limited.

You have to understand that this unit was brand new, with ten completely self-contained flats with support staff on site in the office downstairs from 9.00 a.m. till 6.00 p.m. At all other times there would be security on the doors and each flat was fitted out with everything a mother-to-be would need: brand-new furniture and electrical equipment and cookers and fridges and heating and baby stuff as well. Everything, even down to toilet rolls and toothbrushes. No wonder there was a long list of girls trying to get in. I wanted it. It would be perfect – somewhere safe where I could have my baby and support staff to help in case I had any problems afterwards. Don't forget, I knew nothing about newborn babies and I didn't have any family to advise me either. I had to get in. I just had to!

The housing association said I'd need to hand back the flat in Noel Road if I was successful and that might be a point in my favour. If I got into the unit, the council would get back a flat to house someone else on the waiting list. But it wouldn't be Alice and Emily. I was racked with guilt over this, just like before, but I had to consider my own child now. I thought and thought about it and maybe there was another solution – maybe I could get them to take Alice into the unit as well? So I made applications for both of us. I made my own application in my new name and filled out all the paperwork and explained all the circumstances, and I got letters of support from my doctor and my counsellor and even managed to get the refuge staff to recommend me. Alice's application was more difficult because she wasn't pregnant and she already had her child – but I had to make sure she got in as well.

We were both invited for a formal interview so our needs could be assessed. When the day came, I prayed that we'd be accepted. Alice and I went into the interview together and I gave it everything I had. I told them about my fear of being a bad mother because of what had happened to me when I was three and about my counselling and about the future I wanted for my daughter. I told them how I believed being a resident in the unit would enable me to be a more complete person. I even cried, and that was a minor miracle, because I never cried. I'd coached Alice about what to say and do before we went in. She explained about the childhood abuse and the domestic violence that had driven her out of her home in the first place, and how she was suffering from depression and was going to seek counselling, like me. She explained that she and her child would be homeless if I went into the unit alone, because the authorities refused to register her due to a technicality. I joined in and told them that we'd been together ever since we came to Birmingham and to split us up now might cause emotional damage to either or both of us, and even Emily. She started crying – it was easy for her, she was always doing it – and she said I was her role model and she looked up to me and was guided by me. We pulled out every card we had and we were practically on our knees, begging. But it would be worth it if we could get away from Noel Road.

I received a letter within a week. I'd been accepted. What's more, Alice had been accepted too. I thanked God so sincerely.

It was the end of winter when I moved into the mother and baby unit and I was about four or five months pregnant. It was two giant Victorian houses that had been converted into ten self-contained flats – eight one-bedroom and two two-bedroom – and an office area on the ground floor. The flat itself was big, on the first floor at the front of the building, with a lovely bay window in the living room that looked out on to a park. There was a small hallway, a bathroom and shower, a large bedroom and a small, galley-type kitchen. Money was still tight, so I couldn't buy much when I moved in, but I didn't really need to. The first thing I did buy, however, was flowers. It might seem extravagant, but I wanted the place to be a real home, like I'd never had before in my life. I bought a vase and put the flowers right in the window of the living room and, even now, it gives me a happy feeling when I think of it. My only other extravagance was a cheap stereo I bought from a second-hand shop. I didn't have a television and that didn't matter, but I couldn't live without my music.

Alice was given a two-bedroom flat right opposite me. When I opened my front door, hers was facing me and I later wished she hadn't been so close. To the right was a stairwell that led up to the next floor and down to the office. We had pre-payment meters for electricity, and gas was included in the service charge which was deducted directly from my social security. The support staff frowned on men being in the flats too often, but they also wanted to encourage the fathers to be part of their children's lives and it was a difficult balance knowing who was actually a father and who was just a boyfriend or an opportunist trying to take advantage. That didn't affect me because I wasn't seeing much of Marco and that was all right. To be alone and away from all the insanity seemed so perfect.

So perfectly perfect.

I was so relieved to get away from Noel Road and all the drinking and drug-taking that was going on there. It was the little things that made the biggest difference, like walking barefoot on a carpet, having a hoover to keep the place clean and a washing machine for my clothes, even though I didn't have many of those. I walked out of Noel Road with nothing, just as I'd walked in, and it was like moving from a cave to a castle. I was skinny from never having much food to eat, but now I decided to build myself up, for the sake of the baby. I ate and ate and ate – I was constantly hungry. I was drinking three pints of milk a day and waking up during the night to eat porridge. The food tasted so good, like it had never tasted before. It was almost a compulsion. I couldn't get enough. And I got bigger and bigger. I couldn't afford proper maternity clothes and I put on so much weight I had to wear men's stuff – big polo shirts from Primark and things like that, anything I could get in XXL sizes.

Moseley, where the flat was located, was a new area of Birmingham to be explored. It was a hippy-type locality, with wine bars and trendy pubs and restaurants and Victorian houses converted into luxury flats. It was kind of like the place to be. It was sure of itself and postured up and down its streets. But it also had its down-and-outs and there was some sort of 'care-in-the-community' programme in place for people with mental health issues. Some of the houses had also been converted into hostels for drug and alcohol abusers and whenever I passed by there was always a group of addict-looking people outside. But it didn't detract from the bohemian ambience. There was a picturesque little church and local shops and it all seemed like the most positive place in the world to me. Everything was bright and shiny and I felt that things had finally changed for me and the future had something to offer. I was moving towards the light of normality again.

Marco came by sometimes and stayed for a while and we talked, but it was clear he wasn't interested in the baby, so meeting him became rarer and rarer; and, to be honest, I wasn't all that interested. I made it clear that he was the only one allowed into my flat and he couldn't bring any of his friends with him. The place was for me and my baby and no one else. Alice was allowed in with Emily, of course, but she couldn't bring drink or drugs with her. I was lucky to get this place and it wasn't going to turn into a dosshouse like the previous flat. I'd seen so much of the ugly side of life in the refuge and at Noel Road that now

I just wanted to be left alone. I believed I could make a better life for my daughter if I got rid of all the negative influences that had followed me around like a cloud of flies and hovered over my head. I had different priorities now and I wasn't going back to the old ways for anything or anybody.

Marco didn't like the fact that I allowed no alcohol into the flat. He said I'd changed since I got pregnant and I didn't want to have fun any more, that all I cared about was the baby. And I suppose he was right. But I also wanted my daughter to have a father. I didn't want to deprive her of that. It didn't matter if we weren't living together or if I didn't love him or if he didn't love me, I just thought she should know who he was and have the opportunity to be with him and be part of his life. I hoped he might love her as much as I did when she was born and she would grow up knowing she was loved and wanted by both of us. I didn't want her to think she was an accident or the result of a brief fling, but a precious gift from God.

The whole point of the unit was to teach expectant young mothers how to care for their children and to be able to live independently. I was allocated four hours of direct support every week. I was given an initial interview to assess my needs, together with a diary and a plan of action. My personal support worker came round to my flat in one-hour increments to work through the plan of action and make an agenda for the next support session. It entailed things like getting grants to buy stuff for the baby and filling in forms for a variety of purposes – including getting re-housed. The procedure was, the support staff would issue a notice to quit when they felt we were ready and the council would re-house us in the outside world. The staff maintained the electric meters and we went to them to buy the credits – it was aimed at teaching us how to budget for ourselves. They also came with us if we needed outside help with legal or medical or other issues. I thought it was brilliant: I had my very own support worker and my counsellor at the doctor's, who I continued to see, and I really appreciated all the help these people were giving me, which I wasn't sure I even deserved.

However, I seemed to be alone in this grateful acknowledgement. Most of the other girls didn't seem interested in the support side of the unit and were only there because everything was provided for them. We were all first-time expectant mothers, apart from Alice, and none of us had any idea of the responsibility and pressure of bringing up a baby alone and managing a tenancy and maintaining a proper lifestyle. These things were not instinctive and they had to be learned. If we didn't learn, then we'd fail and end up back in a refuge or hostel. I saw so many girls like that, living like yo-yos – given a place to live and fend for themselves, but who couldn't make it work and gave up and had to go back to the hostel. I always thought that might have been acceptable for girls on their own with no one depending on them, but when you have children you need to try harder, for their sake!

As I settled into life at the unit, I started to see things from the outside – objectively – and the distance between me and the other mothers-to-be grew. When I was in the refuge, and even Noel Road, it felt like I was part of something I couldn't change and I didn't try to. But something different was happening to me now: my mind seemed to be opening like the petals of a flower, and I wasn't on the inside of that institutionalized mentality any more. I'd chosen to step away from it and I could see it more clearly. This was a huge part of my education as a mother. It's not something I could ever have learned from a book or a manual, it had to be experienced! Most of the others drank and smoked weed, even though they were pregnant. Because I wasn't interested in partying and had banned everyone and everything connected with that world from my flat, they considered me to be boring and a live-in babysitter. When Alice realized I wasn't going to continue living that kind of lifestyle, she made friends with the others and carried on as before. And I didn't have a problem with that – until they started bringing their troubles to my door.

I soon found out that the mother and baby unit wasn't going to be the peaceful haven I'd imagined. All the girls in there had suffered really bad abusive or incestuous lives and I was beginning to realize that some people out there were a lot worse than my family. They might have been overprotective and controlling and allowed me to isolate myself and my problems from them, but they were saints compared to the families of these other girls. And it changed the way I looked at life. I was changing already through the counselling, but this realization that I hadn't had it so bad after all escalated the healing process and exorcised some of the demons. I stopped feeling bitter and thinking I was hard done by and started to be thankful for the good things in my life – there weren't many, but it could have been a hell of a lot worse.

I discovered that the unit wasn't really 'new' per se; instead, it had been thoroughly renovated and renamed, because the old unit it replaced had a bad reputation. The girls before had loads of men in there and the place had a name for being a bit of a 'knocking shop'. I began to notice stray men hanging about outside, just like the massage parlour near the refuge. When you have some place that's full of damaged women, whether mothers or not, it will inevitably attract opportunistic and unscrupulous men. The unit was no exception. These people would come round after the support staff left in the evening and we were instructed to call the police if anyone broke in. But some of the girls liked the attention and these men brought alcohol and drugs and, if it got violent, that was just something a lot of these girls had always lived with – it was like the air they breathed. It was normality for them – and they couldn't be made to bring charges against their abusers and manipulators if they didn't choose to.

The office area was manned by a security guard at night, but he just told his mates about the girls in the unit and, when they turned up, he let them in – a whole gang of them once, who tried to get into every single flat in the block. They knocked on the doors and, if the girls opened them, they pushed their way in. I refused to open my door and they started spraying a fire extinguisher in underneath it. I made a complaint the next day and the guy was moved on somewhere else, but the next one was just as bad.

One evening I went to the window to pull the curtains. I was in my dressing gown and was startled to see a man standing right outside. He was directly underneath my window and he began calling to me and whistling and throwing small stones at the glass to attract my attention. I pulled the curtains across and withdrew. Then I could hear all the buzzers going off and someone opening the main security door. Within seconds he was outside my flat, knocking. I didn't answer.

'Let me in.'

'Go away!'

'Come on, I just want to talk for a bit.'

'I'm not interested.'

'I'll take you out.'

'I'm calling the police.'

'Slag! Lesbian! Whore!'

He left after kicking the door and I could hear him slamming around outside. I went back to crocheting my blanket. I didn't have a television, so I knitted, drew pictures, did crosswords and listened to the radio, while the others went out clubbing and drinking and smoking weed and entertaining men. They thought I was crazy. I thought I was starting to regain my sanity.

The girl in the flat above me always had men in there, and they were usually violent. I'd hear them arguing with her but I didn't get involved. But then it got worse, with one particular guy. I could hear him shouting at her and hitting her and things getting broken and her screaming. I called the police. But, by the time they got there, she said she was fine and didn't want anyone involved. So I didn't bother to call them again. The violence kept happening and I asked the office to do something, but they said they couldn't. They gave me the number of the girl's mother and I called her. She wasn't interested and the abuse carried on. Eventually, she lost her baby and she was emotionally crushed. Her body wasn't strong enough for the pregnancy due to the drugs this man had given her and because he'd also put her on the game. She was ordered by the doctor to have a contraceptive implant and she couldn't try for another baby for five years. She was devastated. All she wanted was something to love, that would love her back. Just like me. What she got was a man who destroyed her. Some would say it was her own fault, that she was the architect of her own destiny. I'd say she was conditioned from an early age to accept that level of violence and intimidation in her life – to believe it was normal. To seek it out.

There was another girl in one of the flats in the next-door building who'd had an extremely bad life. Her mother was a prostitute and her father was a pimp. She was adopted when she was young, but her father somehow managed to get her back and, when she was old enough, he sold her out. She was pregnant when she came into the unit and heavily into drink and drugs. One day I was downstairs in the office with the support worker and this girl came screaming in. She slammed the door and locked it behind her, then slid down on to the floor in a heap. Her face was marked, as if she'd been hit, and I could see she was in pain. Next thing, I could hear this guy outside the door calling and cursing her. Then – *BANG!* The door was shaking on its hinges and it's a good thing it was a fire door or it would have come crashing in. *BANG!* again. *BANG!* again. *BANG!* again.

'I'm gonna get you, you slag!'

BANG! again. *BANG!* again. He was trying to kick it in. The girl was hysterical and the support worker shouted that she was calling the police. But he didn't stop. *BANG! BANG! BANG!*

Then it all went quiet, apart from the girl's distraught sobbing. The support worker wouldn't open the door until the police came and by that time the man was gone. When I came out of the office, I could see dents in the outside of the fire door and a smashed chair that he'd been using to try to get in. God knows what would have happened if he had. How could she have survived such a frenzied attack? She went into labour three months early. Her baby was born tiny and needed special care.

On a personal level, I'd realized for some time that Marco had a serious drink and drugs problem and that he'd do anything to get the funds to sustain his habits. He even asked me to sell cannabis for him and to marry someone for money so they could get into the country. I was sick of him now and wanted him to just go and leave me alone. But he kept coming back. I was carrying his child, so I still felt connected to him, but that connection was growing weaker and less important every day. I was with Marco for a year, until Alyssia was born. It was on and off. I knew in my heart it wasn't going to be permanent and I didn't want it to be. I just needed something to love, something to give meaning and purpose to my life, and he was there. In the appropriate place at the appropriate time. But when I had the baby, all the feelings of loneliness and sadness left and were replaced with love and excitement and an overwhelming will to live.

Marco went into prison for drink-driving the day I went into labour. I woke at 2.00 a.m. on 21 August 2003 with pains running through my stomach – nothing major, but they were consistent. I waited to see if they lasted, just in case it was a false alarm. They did, and started increasing in frequency. I wasn't worried about the pain that much; I was going to have my baby and I was full of excitement. I took a taxi to the hospital at 10.00 a.m. After examining me, the midwife said I wasn't even dilated yet and sent me home. By the afternoon, I was in serious pain and took another taxi to the hospital. Again, they told me I wasn't dilated and I should go back home. But I had no more money for taxis and I could feel my body going into spasm. I persuaded them to give me a bed and I waited.

There were no complications and Alyssia was ready to come when she was due, in the early hours of 22 August. They gave me a shot of Pethidine because it was so painful and I lost four hours – I can't remember that stretch of time at all, it just disappeared. When my baby was born, I felt so overwhelmed with rapture. It was the most amazing feeling I'd ever experienced. I was so full of love for this little girl who'd just come into the world, this tiny thing that would need me and I'd have to be the best I could because that's what she deserved. I swore to myself there and then that nothing would ever come between me and my daughter. Even now, I cannot find the words to express the enormous love I felt for her. She was everything to me – and still is.

I have low white platelets so my blood is very thin and when I cut myself, I bleed a lot. I did tell the nurses this but they were too busy to take much notice. After the placenta came, they were supposed to give me an injection to help stop any haemorrhaging, but they didn't and there was blood all over the place. They told me I needed to get up and shower and, when I tried, I collapsed. They then needed to take a urine sample, so they gave me a little bucket thing to pee in. Before I could even go, I filled the bucket with blood and it was overflowing. I had to go and lie down. A nurse gave me an injection and I passed out for a while. The next day the midwife said I should be up and walking about or I'd get thrombosis and I thought, 'Thrombosis – I'll be lucky if I've got any blood *left*!' The food tasted terrible, so I put Alyssia in the nursery and went down to the hospital shop to get something to eat. I passed out again on the way back up in the lift and came to with some man trying to get me on to a bed in the hallway. The nurses did some tests and discovered I had severe anaemia, and I was put on a course of iron tablets.

Marco and I had already split up by then, but I thought he had the right to see his daughter. I didn't have a visiting order, he never sent me one, but I telephoned the prison and they said I could come and visit under special circumstances. I travelled up to Liverpool on the train with the baby, but they then refused to let me in because I didn't have a visiting order. Eventually, after much begging and pleading, I was able to convince them that I'd made an arrangement over the telephone. I had to go through all the degrading entry routines like metal detectors and sniffer dogs and patting down, and they applied some chemical stuff to my hands to see if I'd been in contact with drugs. They even made me change Alyssia's nappy and use one they gave me, and at last I was shown into the visiting room with the other families. When they brought the prisoners in, Marco looked terrible, like he was in withdrawal or something, and he wasn't all that happy to see me. He didn't want to know his daughter and he wouldn't even hold her. He looked edgy and not like the funny and amusing guy he was when I first met him. Then he asked me if I could bring some cannabis in for him, hidden in the baby carrier, and said I could pass it to him from mouth to mouth when we kissed. I couldn't believe what I was hearing – it hurt me so much. He wanted me to risk my freedom and use his own child to get him a bit of marijuana. If I'd been anywhere else I would've hit him. I just stood up and walked out and I never went back to visit him again. Whatever feelings I might have had left for him were gone. I had my beautiful daughter, who had come into my life and made it important again. I had no need of him any more.

My community service had been put on hold while I was pregnant, but now I still had it hanging over me. After Alyssia was born, I was sent a letter to attend court again. I took my support worker with me and prepared what I was going to say about having had a breakdown and that I was seeking treatment and trying to rebuild my life. The magistrates were as unimpressed as they were the first time I appeared in court.

'Can't your support worker look after your child while you complete your hours?'

'No one's looking after my baby except me.'

I was trying to control my anger. Just because these

people were born better off than me and had had more opportunities given to them in life, they thought they could play God with *my* life. But I was adamant that Mother Teresa herself wasn't good enough for me to leave my baby with. And there wasn't a law in the land that said I had to!

'You have to complete your community order.'

'You might as well put me in prison now, because I'm not leaving her with anyone!'

And I thought they were going to. They huffed and they puffed pompously up on their podium and they lectured me again on the seriousness of the crime of giving food away to the poor that wasn't mine to give. And then they fined me another £250 and dropped the community order.

The fines were deducted from my social security payments.

14
Mother

When I came home after having Alyssia, I felt so ill I couldn't eat – and when I did, I couldn't keep the food down. I went from fifteen to nine stone weight in about four months. My hair started to fall out and my nails were breaking. I was exhausted all the time and would fall asleep as if I was narcoleptic. I was like a balloon that had deflated – that was sagging. That's just how I felt. The change in me was so dramatic, when I went to my doctor's surgery they didn't recognize me. For me to be able to eat again and keep the food down, I had to take in a little and often, small things like crackers or toast to begin with. I had to build up to having a full meal. They told me my anaemia had affected my appetite and it would be a slow road to recovery.

This was a time when Alice showed the goodness of her real nature and she helped me as much as she could. She could be so kind when she wanted to be and had an endearing as well as a self-destructive side to her. Her violent boyfriend hadn't followed her to the unit and, one day when I'd recovered enough to go shopping in town, we were served by a good-looking guy and Alice went all cutesy and coy, which wasn't like her at all. Later, she told me she fancied the man, but he was different to the usual people she spoke to on the street and she didn't know how to approach him. Next time I was in the shop, he served me again and I thought I'd play cupid. It would be good for Alice if she could get a regular, decent boyfriend and not the violent dopeheads she usually attracted.

'You remember the girl who came in with me last time?'

'Yes.'

'Well . . . she really likes you.'

'Does she?'

He said he liked her too and he gave me his phone number so she could ring him. He seemed really nice and really normal and I thought this could be the break Alice needed in life to get her back into society. I turned to go with the phone number – then turned back.

'You're not married, are you?'

'No.'

'Do drugs?'

'No.'

'Drink?'

'A little.'

I sounded like her mother. We laughed. I knew he would treat her well, and Emily too.

They started seeing each other, but after some time I began to hear arguing coming from Alice's flat. I thought to myself, 'Oh no, not another wrong 'un.' What had I done! It got very bad one night and I thought I'd better go over there and see if she was all right. If he was beating her up, then I had to stop it, seeing as it was me who'd brought them together. When I went across, I found her beating him up, not the other way round. He was backed into a corner and she was throwing everything in the place at him. I couldn't believe it. When I came in, it created enough of a diversion for him to get out. He never came back.

'What was all that about, Alice?'

'He was getting on my nerves.'

'Why?'

'I don't know!'

I believe she'd become so used to being treated badly, it was all she could relate to, all she could understand. When a decent man came along, she couldn't deal with the normality of the relationship, because it wasn't normal to her. It was alien to her and she found it more threatening than the violence.

Alice continued to get into trouble at the mother and baby unit. While I was pregnant and not going out anywhere, I'd helped her by babysitting a few times for Emily. I loved the little girl and felt sorry for her, and she was the reason I did so much for Alice. Had Alice not had Emily, I would've left her to her own devices long ago. But the babysitting became expected rather than a favour and, when Alyssia was born, I had to say no – even though it hurt me to do that because I knew she'd only leave Emily with someone else. She, like Marco, said I'd become 'boring' and was no fun any more, and she hooked up with the other girls at the unit who had similar social interests. But they were immature and bitchy and were always falling out with each other over trivial things: 'she said and he said and they said what you said', that kind of thing. Alice and another girl had a falling-out and the thing was escalating. I told her I didn't want to get involved, as it was none of my business, so she went off in a huff and tried to rally some of the other girls for support. They split into two factions, with some on Alice's side and some on the other girl's side, and it was brewing up to a showdown.

It all exploded one evening outside my front door. The other girl and her friends came to have it out. However, Alice's faction didn't show up and she was all alone. I could hear the commotion outside, but I kept telling myself it was none of my business and I should stay out of it. Then I heard Alice banging on my door.

'Shelley! Shelley!'

I wanted to ignore her, I really did. But how could I? We'd been through a lot together and I couldn't leave her out there to face it on her own. Alyssia was asleep in her cot, so I went out the flat door and locked it behind me. The other girl was screaming like a banshee and brandishing a golf club. There were three others with her and they had weapons in their hands as well, but I can't remember what – maybe sticks or something. And there was Alice, right outside my door, shouting back at them. I didn't go out there to fight her corner because I'd come to the conclusion that Alice liked the drama. She wanted to fight and scream and she wanted all the stress release that came with it. I didn't know who was right or wrong, but I couldn't sit inside my flat and let her get beaten up either – even if that's what she wanted.

When she saw me coming out, Alice went for the other girl and it was off. I can't remember exactly what happened next because the adrenaline was pumping and it was fight or flight. I know I was trying to get Alice out of there, so I must have decided flight was the better option. I pushed her backwards until she came against her own front door, which was open, and Emily was looking out, crying. Then I manoeuvred her into the flat and shut the door after her. While this was happening, I was being kicked and hit and my hair pulled from behind. I don't think it was intentional or they wanted to beat me up, it was Alice they were after and I was in their way. But now she was safe inside with her door locked and I was outside and turning to face them.

When I did turn, they stopped and didn't try it with me. I was the quiet one in the unit and wasn't involved in any of their catty vendettas. But they still looked threatening. I put my hands up.

'I'm not getting involved.'

'You just did.'

'Because you're outside my door and my baby's sleeping.'

'Oh . . . sorry . . .'

'Just take it somewhere else.'

They moved aside for me and I went back into my flat and swore I'd never get involved again. I could hear them swearing at Alice through her door for a few seconds and then they went away.

Alice never really got over that fight with the other unit girl. I knew we were growing apart and things couldn't ever be the same between us again. I bought her an orange juice one day and she said I'd opened it and was insinuating I'd put something in it to poison her. I came to the conclusion she'd had such a bad life that she created crises to get attention. But now she seemed like she was losing it completely. Maybe she thought I should have backed her up more, but I was on the outside of it all by then, looking in. Alice courted disaster, she wanted to fight and argue, and I just wanted a quiet life. She began to think everyone had turned against her. I don't think they had, but I wasn't part of her scene any more so I can't say for sure. Then she was seeing some man and he left her for the girl who'd come screaming into the office that day. I don't think it helped her perception of herself and, in the end, she started acting more and more strangely.

She got depressed and couldn't be bothered to take Emily to school, so I used to walk the little girl there and back every day. It was a half-hour trek each way and Alice just took it for granted and never seemed to care one way or the other. She was getting really aggressive-paranoid about everything by now and I thought it might be the long-term effect of all the weed she smoked. She'd been allowed back on the housing list by then and was offered a two-bedroom flat not far away. I went up there every day with Alyssia and helped her decorate and wallpaper the place and then I'd go back to the mother and baby unit. Then one day I went round and she wouldn't answer the door to me. I rang, but she didn't return my call. I wrote her a letter, but she never replied.

And that was the end of it.

In a way, I was relieved. Marco was gone and now Alice was gone too and I was truly on my own. Except for Alyssia. And she was all I needed.

Then I got a letter from the Salvation Army. They'd sent it to the Department for Work and Pensions, to be forwarded to the person with my national insurance number. I'd tried to change my NI number but couldn't and I knew it was now the only way I could be traced. The letter said they were trying to contact a person called Shelley Mackenney and if that was me they'd appreciate it if I got in touch with them. If it wasn't me, then apologies, etc. They didn't mention anything about my family, but I knew it was them. I tore the letter up and threw it away.

But the past was beginning to close in on me. During my counselling, it was suggested that I should consider making contact with my mother so I could confront my demons – or one of them, at least. They managed to get me a phone number, I don't know how. I didn't ask. I held on to the number for a long time, but didn't call because I wasn't sure it was something I wanted to do. What if she told my dad? But then, they already knew I was in Birmingham, they just didn't know where. I was afraid. The fears I had when I was pregnant, that I would never be good enough for my daughter, were very real. So real they were obsessive. Since Alyssia's arrival, those fears had abated, but I didn't know what effect meeting my mother would have on them. Maybe they'd come back again. Maybe her indifference would rub off on me – contaminate me – if I touched her.

There was a large focus on my mother in counselling and on what it meant to be a mother. I'd had the feeling I knew my daughter before I'd even met her. And I wondered if it was the same for my mother – did she feel like that when she was pregnant with me? Did she ever love me? Did she ever think about me? Did she regret what happened? Did she wonder what things could have been like? Would she recognize me if she saw me now?

Questions. Questions. Questions.

But no answers.

I was so excited about meeting my own daughter, I couldn't help looking back to the past. And that's when a memory came to me that I didn't even know I had.

I'm six years old and my father is taking me somewhere. We're in his car and I love being in his car. He drives very fast sometimes and it's exciting. He's an exciting man to be with – like a movie star or something. We go over the river and drive north through London. We go to a house and a woman is there. I don't know who she is, but I think I should know her. I'm looking up at her and she's looking down at me and it's like there's something between us – something invisible, like a glass wall or something. Even though I know there's nothing there. That's what it seems like to me. I'm smiling, but she's not. There's no expression on her face. She doesn't speak to me, even though I keep smiling. The woman is a lot shorter than my father and she has long blonde hair and blue eyes. She's speaking to my father, but her words are far off and so are his – deep and hollow, like in slow motion. I don't understand all the words, just some of them. I understand one thing the woman says:

'Tell her to come back when she's sixteen.'

That's all. They're the only words I can understand. The rest are grumbly and growly – stumbling, bumbling words. We don't stay long and my father takes me to a burger bar afterwards, for a treat. Because the woman wasn't friendly. I think he feels sorry for me or something, but I don't know why.

To tell the truth, never in his life did my dad say anything bad about my mother. In fact, he always told me how much she loved me. And maybe it would have been better if he'd said she hated me. Then I'd have been able to understand. But to love someone and still leave them, that's what I couldn't get straight in my mind. I loved Alyssia and I knew I could never ever leave her. So why?

Eventually, it got the better of me and I finally summoned up the nerve to ring the number. It was so strange, because I didn't know what to call her. 'Mum' was an alien word to me. I couldn't get my tongue round it. I tried, but it wouldn't come out of my mouth. I remembered, when I was growing up, hating Mother's Day. I hated watching my schoolmates making cards and I hated going to the shops and seeing all the novelty stuff with 'Best Mum in the World' written all over it. I was jealous of the other kids and the relationships they had with their mothers – good or bad. I felt cheated of that mother/daughter thing that seemed so important and precious. So I didn't call her anything.

'Hello.'

'Hello.'

'It's Shelley.'

'Shelley?'

'Your daughter.'

I could feel the surprise at the other end of the phone line. I could touch her trepidation. Some small talk followed. Nothing deep. Nothing meaningful. What do you say to a stranger who's your mother?

'I'm in Birmingham.'

'Are you? What are you doing up there?'

'I have a baby.'

'You can't come live with me.'

'What?'

'I don't have the room.'

Why did she say that? I didn't want to live with her. I felt offended, even insulted. Like I was begging for something from her. I didn't need her hospitality or empathy or sympathy. I was only making conversation. After some more strained small talk she asked, to my surprise, if she could come up and meet me. It was she who suggested it, not me. I was worried at first, in case she told my family where I was. But I knew she hated my father and my nan, and the chances were she wouldn't have had any contact with them. The urge to see her was too great and I agreed. I don't know why she wanted to come up, maybe it was out of curiosity – or maybe guilt. I really couldn't tell.

I remember looking out the window on the day she was to arrive and feeling all funny inside. It was a confusion of feelings: excitement at seeing her for the first time in so long and fear that maybe I'd be a disappointment to her. She didn't want me before, why should she want to know me now, after all the mistakes I'd made? I felt guilt too – here I was waiting for my mother, while Nan, who was my spiritual mother, didn't know what had become of me and was probably worried out of her mind. Finally, I felt apprehension – was I doing the right thing? Would I feel better or worse for doing it? I'd imagined this day all through my growing up. I'd anticipated it, longed for it. I could see it in my mind: we'd both be smiling and crying at the same time and we'd rush into each other's arms and tell each other how much we loved each other and how we'd never be apart again.

She came with another woman, a little old lady with white hair, and introduced her as my grandmother. My other grandmother. The meeting was cold. Stilted. She didn't want to run to me and I couldn't bring myself to run to her. She didn't smile through her tears and she didn't hurry to hug me. There were no tears at all, from either of us. No warmth. No love. No connection. We were strangers who barely looked at each other. She was shorter than me, with blonde hair, wearing black jeans and T-shirt. Neither of us said anything at first, because neither of us could think of anything to say. I was expecting to feel some magnetism, some attraction, some affinity even. Some tenderness tugging at my heartstrings. I expected to feel like everything that was broken in my life had been fixed and the sun would peep out from behind the confused clouds.

'I don't like what you're wearing.'

They were the first words she spoke to me. I could scarcely believe it. I was in a hostel, for God's sake, broke, just had a baby, emotionally twisted – and she passed a comment on my clothes. I felt like saying in return, 'So this is what having a mother is like,' but I didn't.

Something that I'd hoped would be so right was going so wrong. She didn't feel like my mother. The magic I'd expected wasn't there. I felt cheated, as if they'd kept my real mother in London and sent up an imposter instead. Someone I didn't recognize. Nothing was mended and the spiritual sun wasn't shining. I wondered if she could see the deflated expression on my face and I wished I'd never made contact with her. I asked both of them to sit down and offered them a cup of tea.

'I can see you take after your father.'

I assumed she was talking about my height.

'Do I?'

'Yes, and I'd like to stick a knife in him.'

I can't really remember much of what followed. I didn't introduce Alyssia to her as her granddaughter and she didn't ask to be introduced. I was protective of my daughter and this woman might hurt her emotionally like she hurt me, so I didn't want them to get to know each other. There was more small talk about this and that and nothing much and even less than nothing. Then I asked her about the night she walked out of the house and left me on my own. I expected this to catch her by surprise and shake her out of her nonchalance and detachment.

'Nothing would have stopped me leaving that night.'

'Why?'

'It was over.'

'What was?'

'Your father and me. I have no regrets about walking away.'

'What about me? I was only three.'

'I know.'

She never said sorry or that she loved me or missed me or thought about me, or that she even felt anything for me. She did say she was happy I was born a girl because my father wanted a boy. I was getting angry and about to lose my cool. The old woman spoke.

'It's depressing in here. Can we go out somewhere?'

'Yes, I think so. Shelley?'

'Where?'

'We could go and get something to eat.'

I didn't want to go with them, but I did. I dressed Alyssia and we all walked to a nearby restaurant. I was feeling hurt and emotional, but I tried to hide it – I didn't want her to see me hurting. We ate, with more small talk about even less than before, then we went to Mothercare and she bought some things for Alyssia. The two women talked between themselves and I said hardly anything at all. I was relieved when they left – I could finally succumb to the disappointment I'd been hiding all afternoon. I don't know what I'd expected. Not what I got, that's for sure. So, what *did* I expect? That I'd look like her? That she'd look like me? That she'd say she was sorry for leaving me? That I'd say I was sorry for not being able to stop her? The thing that affected me more than anything else was the coldness, the lack of feeling – not in her for me, but in me for her!

She was unfeeling and it didn't bother her. But my own apathy troubled me. Was I like her after all? Were my worst fears being realized? It frightened me: of all the things in the world I didn't want to happen, I didn't want to become like my mother. I thought about the visit after she left. I thought maybe I shouldn't be blaming her for everything. Maybe she felt as alienated as I did. Could she have sensed my bitterness? I tried to turn it off while she was with me, but I couldn't do it completely. Some of it still showed, I was sure. I'd carried my issues around with me for years – wore them like a crown of thorns – and I couldn't let go of them just like that! She may have had the best of intentions, but instead of being receptive, I was defensive and suspicious. I couldn't help it. I didn't have enough trust to open my heart and let her into it again. It was too big a risk. The counselling had made me address how I felt and showed me how to deal with it, but I still couldn't banish it – I could only try to manage it. I was bitter because I felt she owed me something for making me feel unwanted all these years and she wasn't paying out. She defaulted. And, after she left, I felt like I'd been abandoned all over again. I was back in the dark room in that dark house and I was crying. Crying for someone to come and save me. Then Alyssia stirred and made a sound.

And I smiled again.

The clouds passed over and the sun shone.

I was never going to be able to build bridges with my mother – she didn't seem to want to and I didn't seem to be able to. In a way, it gave me closure. I never wondered why she didn't love me after that because I didn't care. She didn't mean so much any more. I vowed to dedicate my life to my daughter. It didn't matter what had happened in the past – the future was all that mattered now.

I never rang my mother again.

Alyssia

Before I left the mother and baby unit, they asked me to do a painting for them that would represent what they were all about at an elemental level. I'd painted the whole of the bedroom where Alyssia and I slept as a Hundred Acre Wood mural, like in *Winnie-the-Pooh*. I painted everything: the walls, the windowsills, the light switch, the skirting boards, the door and the ceiling. The wood was populated with fairytale characters. Hansel and Gretel skipped secretly with their basket of breadcrumbs and Rapunzel's long hair came tumbling down from the treetops; Snow White bit into a blood-red apple and Rumpelstiltskin spun gold in the gloaming. When the door was closed, it disappeared into the ambience and we were surrounded by trees and the magic of make-believe, and it was all ours. There was no way in for anyone else. Just us. Two babes in the wood.

I took inspiration for the unit's picture from the mural I was involved with at community service. I painted a border of different hands — black and white and brown and yellow and red — all holding on to each other's wrists so it looked like a chain that went round the picture, with flowers and plants growing gaily in between. In the middle was the silhouette of a city against a skyline and in front of that was an assortment of different people – white, black, Muslim, Sikh, disabled people, children – all holding hands. They hung it in the foyer of the main office and I've been told it's still there today!

I was able to do it because my head was in a good place. I'd never before or since felt anything like the rush of love I had when Alyssia was born. I knew from that moment onwards that life could throw what it liked at me, but nothing would ever stop me loving my daughter. Nothing would ever stop me from being there for her. I would never leave her and I would tell her every day that I loved her. It wasn't just because those were things I never had from my mother, but because she didn't ask to be brought into the world and she deserved to know what it felt like to be wanted.

I can say without a doubt in my mind that the single thing that saved me from myself was my daughter, Alyssia. Before she was born, I was truly lost. I didn't know what I was doing or where I was going. I had no sense of belonging – no home, no happiness, no past and no future. I'd lost everything I knew and nearly lost my mind as well. I was living in darkness and depression. I'd given up on ever being able to function normally again. I was truly broken. When Alyssia came into the world, she brought something with her that I'd never experienced before – it was like the sound of laughter being blown along on the breeze and you can hear it and it gives you hope. Or the sun coming out from behind the clouds or the moonshadow that runs before you on a clear night, like an elusive longing. It was magical, what I felt for her.

It was pure and untainted. It gave me an incentive to change, to put myself back together – better than before. Stronger, more resilient.

I was determined to build a life for me and her. I'd met my own mother and finally the fear inside me that I'd be like her had dissipated – the obsession of her had faded from my mind. Every time I looked at my daughter I knew I would *never* be like my mother – I would kill myself rather than ever leave her. I'd be the mother on all those novelty items in the shop windows, 'The Best Mum in the World'. All the things I'd been through since I'd run away would teach me how to behave like a human being. Alyssia wouldn't be a hostel kid like Emily, she wouldn't have to experience the drugs and the drink and the men and the fighting and the fear. It was the fear in the innocent eyes of some of those children that was most heartbreaking. Not understanding what was happening to them, not knowing what they'd done to deserve it. She would never be left with strangers, never be traumatized, never have to absorb the abuse and believe it to be normal.

When I was pregnant, I thought about all the things I would need to change once Alyssia was born. I'd no longer be on my own, without responsibility for anyone but myself. I knew that. My daughter would have to be taken into account with everything I did. Marco was gone and she wouldn't have a father to fall back on, like some lucky girls do. Someone to be strong for her and spoil her – a dad for her to be his little princess. I'd have to be both, mother and father. It frightened me. Would I be able to cope alone, to be there day and night and deal with everything, every need she'd have? Would I have what it takes? I'd have the love, that much I knew, but would it be enough? I promised myself it would be. And I took that promise seriously.

Then she was born and I was born again with her. I remembered that time when I'd left her in her cot in the nursery to go down to the hospital shop and I'd passed out in the lift – when I got back, she was gone! She wasn't there! I couldn't find her and my heart was racing like a runaway train. Where was she? I ran out of the nursery in sheer terror to the nurses' station and there she was. The midwife had taken her for a weighing. I felt like I was going to faint again with the relief of finding her. I picked her up and held her to my heart and never wanted to let her go. And that must have been how Nan felt when she came to the betting shop at lunchtime that day and I was gone!

Alyssia was the perfect baby. She was happy and content from the minute she was born. The only time she seemed upset was when she was away from me. The health visitor told me I had to put her in her cot at night and leave her to cry, so she'd get used to it. But it broke my heart. I couldn't bear to hear her crying, so I'd pick her up and rock her and let her sleep in bed beside me. I brought her everywhere in a baby carrier until she was six months old. She looked too tiny to be in the big pram all by herself, so I strapped her to me and bought a big fleece duffel coat that wrapped round us both and we were so close it felt like we were one person – that she was an extension of me and not something separate at all. I remember when colic set in and I'd put her in the carrier and walk up and down singing to her and rubbing her back, night after night. I was all alone, with no one else to help me, and I became exhausted. But I kept doing it – night after night after night – until the colic went away.

I've often wondered about reincarnation and if we've been here before. I find it difficult to believe that we can know all we need to know about the universe in one short lifetime. And it isn't fair, is it? How can it be fair for some people to have such easy lives and others such grief and hardship? I know the churches tell us we'll all be rewarded in heaven – as long as we're good. But I don't buy that. It's easier to be good when you have everything in life. Easier to get into heaven. Harder if you have to lie and cheat and steal just to get by. No, I think we need more than one life to achieve full realization – true perception – profound understanding. To reach the state where we can move on to apotheosis – nirvana – heaven. But even that wouldn't be fair, would it? One sequence of lives is never going to be exactly the same as another sequence of lives; there would always be inequalities. The only way it could possibly be fair is for everyone to experience everything. For everyone to *be* everyone. One plus one plus one plus one equals one. So, when you're good to someone else, you're really being good to yourself.

And when you're bad to someone else –

The reason I mention this is because Alyssia was a strangely perceptive child when she was very young. She used to talk about her big sister who was run over by a truck and about her other mother, the one she used to have before she was born. And one of the biggest problems I had with her during potty training was, she insisted on peeing standing up. She's forgotten it all now, but she used to go into great detail about her other life. She could sense something that was and wasn't there – like the man on the stair.

I never wanted to be apart from my daughter. When she was older, I was offered a half-day place for her at a nursery. I thought about it for a few seconds, then turned it down. I was enjoying my time with her, teaching her everything she needed to know at home. I'm sure this will sound neurotic, but I didn't trust nursery staff. I'd met women who did that job and didn't have any children of their own and who went to work with hangovers and bad hormone days. No, I didn't send her to nursery, but travelled to 'stay and play' centres instead. However, as time went on, I could feel myself falling into the same routine as me and Nan. When I was young, Nan went everywhere with me and rarely let me out of her sight. And that's how it was developing with Alyssia and me.

Déjà vu!

I didn't want my protective nature to stop her from developing as an individual and learning things for herself, and I didn't want her to think later on that she'd missed out because of my insecurities. When these thoughts finally manifested themselves in my mind, I had to stop myself in my tracks and remind myself that she needed to mix with others – nothing bad would happen, despite what my overprotective OCD was saying. It's so hard when you love someone like life itself and all you want is to look after them. But I was overdoing it and there was a danger we'd end up not living at all, but sinking into each other's psyches and becoming fixed for ever in an unhealthy attachment that was similar to the one I'd run away from. We needed to develop together, and I didn't want my daughter to feel trapped, like I had.

I also missed working. I missed the routine of it and earning my own money and having my own independence and self-respect. But I knew I'd miss my daughter more and I didn't trust anyone enough to look after her. I wanted to be a full-time mother for as long as possible and really enjoy the time I spent with her before she grew up. I wanted to be there to pick her up when she fell over, to comfort her when she was sick, to answer all her questions and to be a wall between her and the harsh world. I wouldn't allow drink or drugs near her and I was reluctant to bring people into her life unless I was very sure about them. I didn't want a stepfather for her and kept away from men completely. I didn't want her calling anyone 'Dad' because I believed she had the right to know where she came from and I would never lie to her about her father.

I always tried to make sure we did stuff together when she was growing up. I taught her to knit and crochet and cook and paint and papier mâché. She loved practical things like me and we'd do small experiments together in the kitchen. I was a science ace when I was at school, it was my best subject, so we made volcanoes with bicarbonate of soda, did acid and alkaline tests with red cabbage dye and made boats with little engines on them.

We mixed up cornflour goo that turns hard on impact and then reverts to a liquid, and I was just as big a kid as she was. Reliving my life. Finding the childhood that had eluded me the first time round. I taught her to lead and not follow, not to worry about what other people said, to respect her elders and to make sure she was safe at all times. I was overprotective – I admit it. I couldn't help it. It was my duty to take care of her, like a father would have, and guide her as best I could.

I spent my first Christmas with Alyssia at the mother and baby unit and it was the best time I ever had in my life. I bought a tree and decorations from the second-hand shops – where I got everything – and I made fabric bells and stars and picked wild holly and ivy and made a wreath for the door. I had my first sewing machine when I was ten, so I was quite capable of making stuff and it's a skill that comes in handy when you're very poor. Alyssia was still only a baby and she didn't know what was going on or what it all meant, but for me it was wonderful and I didn't need presents or anything because I had her. I'd saved up a little social security money and I bought a baby walker and a bouncer and a musical thing with lights that projected on to the wall like a turning star-filled sky. I still didn't have a television, so I filled the flat with Christmas music from the radio and I sang carols to her. Alyssia was always happy when I sang; I think she sensed that I was happy too. It was our first Christmas together, we were alone and we were happy in our isolation. I think it was the first time I'd felt real happiness in my life. *Real* happiness – not the thrill you get from shopping or socializing or sex or other superficial stuff like that.

I didn't have much contact with Marco after the prison visit, but I didn't want to sever all connection with him for Alyssia's sake. I always hoped he'd be a father for her, even though I knew deep down he wouldn't. I tried to fool myself and I used to write and tell him how she was doing and send him pictures of her. Eventually I received a letter back from him, along with the pictures. It wasn't very long, only about a page. He told me he was already married, that he had a wife and child back in Italy. He said he'd separated from his wife before he met me, but now they wanted to give the relationship another chance for the sake of their child. He was going back to Italy and this letter was to say goodbye. He never mentioned Alyssia – the child that I'd had, the child he said he wanted, the child he said he'd love. I read the letter while I was standing in the hall and I had to go sit on the edge of the bed to take it in. He was really saying his other child meant more to him than my child. Alyssia was sleeping in her cot at the time and I looked over at her and saw how beautiful she was, how angelic. And I couldn't understand why he wouldn't love her. I didn't want him to love me; I didn't love him. But I'd hoped he'd love her. The letter said he'd be gone by the time I read it.

I never saw him again.

Neither did Alyssia.

I swore then I'd make sure my daughter never felt she'd missed out on her father's love. I'd love her enough for both of us. And I have!

I tried after that to lead by example with my daughter. When she was old enough, I told her I didn't like drink or drugs. I told her pubs were places for men and not ladies and alcohol was bad for her health and it made girls look cheap when they drank too much of it. I didn't know if any of this would work when she grew older, but I had to try. I'd seen what excessive drinking and drug-taking did to women and the effect it had on their innocent children and the emotional damage it did. I also realized Alyssia would learn from what she saw and not necessarily from what I told her, so I had to be her role model. I wanted us to have an open and honest relationship and I tried not to be overbearing because I didn't want her to feel smothered like I had. I tried to make her understand that we're all human and it's easy to make mistakes – God knows I'd made enough of them myself. I wanted her to know I would always be there for her and she could come to me and tell me anything. She need never be afraid, she need never feel alone or misunderstood. She could always come to me for help.

Always!

When she was about a year old, I was approached by a woman in Birmingham city centre. She was going on about how gorgeous Alyssia was and she gave me a card with the name of a child modelling agency she worked for. There was a telephone number and a website address; I looked it up and it was genuine. I called them and they asked me to bring Alyssia along to see them. Then I thought about it and decided against it. Childhood doesn't last all that long and I didn't want to push my daughter into the competitive world of modelling when she should be growing up and discovering all the little important things that kids her age found so fascinating. I decided it would be better to let her make her own choices, when she was old enough.

I didn't want Alyssia to go to nursery, but eventually the time came for her to go to school. I was scared – my little girl was going to school and I wouldn't be there if she needed me. I went in with her on the first day and the teacher said I could stay for an hour or so if Alyssia wanted me to.

'Do you want me to stay, Lissy?'

'No, Mama, you can go.'

She always called me mama, right from the first time she could talk – not mum or mummy or mother, but mama. It's not a name you hear much and she never had friends before she went to school, so I have no idea where it came from. Not from me. Maybe it was something from the other life she talked about.

Anyway, I was shocked for a moment when she said I could go, but then I was pleased. I wanted her to miss me and I didn't want her to miss me, if that makes sense. She'd never had friends her own age and I wanted that for her. She needed little friends, other children to play with, to interact with, to learn from. It had always been me playing with her up till now, but she needed more to stop her getting introverted and isolated. I knew going to school was just what she needed at this stage in her little life, to open up other horizons for her. But I also knew I was going to miss her terribly and the world would seem so forlorn and empty without her there beside me. I didn't know what to do with myself for the first few months, except clean and clean again and then clean what I'd just cleaned. I played my music and sang to it, and of course it wasn't the same without Alyssia singing along with me in her own little-voiced way. But she was happy and adapted to school without any heart-wrenching on her part.

And if she was happy, I was happy.

We had moved from the mother and baby unit to a maisonette (which I'll tell you about in the next chapter) and I remember one day, when Alyssia was about two, I left her playing in the front room and went upstairs to get something from the bedroom. While I was up there, I heard a dog barking in the distance. Normally, this wouldn't be anything strange, but for some reason I just had a shivery feeling about it. I couldn't have been more than a few seconds and, when I came back downstairs, Alyssia was gone. The front door had been locked and the chain on when I went upstairs, but now the door was wide open. I panicked.

'Lissy! Lissy, where are you?'

There was no sign of her along the balcony and the dog was still barking. I ran along the walkway to the stairwell and there she was, halfway down. A little Jack Russell dog was beside her, snarling at anyone who tried to pass or come near her. There were people at the bottom of the stairs, unable to get up, and people at the top, unable to get down.

'Lissy, what are you doing here?'

'The doggie, Mama . . .'

I brought her back to the maisonette and the dog followed. He wouldn't leave her. I took him in and gave him some water and he stayed with us. I made many enquiries, trying to find out who owned him, but they were all unsuccessful. We kept him and called him Tiny. To this day I don't know how Alyssia managed to open the door by herself and get to the stairwell in the short time I was away from her. I do know she has a natural affinity for animals and she always loved visiting Moseley Bog Nature Reserve whenever we could spend time there. Tiny was old when he came to us and eventually he died. But we have another dog now and two cats as well, and they all fight to sleep on the bed with Alyssia. Over the years, she's rescued any hurt animal she came across. As a result, I've had all sorts living with me – rabbits, pigeons, blackbirds and starlings, stray cats and dogs. We'd keep the birds until they recovered and then let them fly away. The RSPCA would come and take the other animals while Alyssia was at school, otherwise I'd have had a zoo in the maisonette – which would have suited her up to the sky. She named every one of them and she kept a diary with pictures of every animal she helped.

It's always been impossible for me to be angry with Alyssia. When I was painting her bedroom deep in the wildwood like before, I noticed tiny little pink footprints leading away from the paint tray. I followed them and found she'd put her hands in the paint and was pressing handprint patterns all round the walls in my bedroom. I believe in artistic expression and I thought the handprints looked quite cute, so I left them. Whenever she did something she thought might make me angry, I'd get that *look* – all big eyes and bottom lip. Then I came across her in front of the mirror practising it! I watched while she tried out various versions until it was perfect. I smiled and said nothing.

I've written about my daughter here because to understand me is to know about her. She came to me at a time when I needed her most. She saved my life.

And I will love her eternally.

16
Moving Again

After being in the mother and baby unit for about fifteen months, I was given notice to quit by the housing association. This was standard procedure. It meant they considered me ready to move on and stand on my own two feet again. It also meant I had to go to the council and ask to be placed on the homeless register once more. I filled out all the forms in my new name and the support workers at the unit gave me a letter of endorsement. It took the council about three months to assess me and, when I was finally accepted, they told me I would be offered the next available place. So I knew it wouldn't be long before I'd have to leave the unit and live independently again. And I wanted that, but I didn't want it to be a repeat of Noel Road. Everything had been provided in the unit, which meant I had nothing to take with me – no furniture or fridge or cooker or cot for Alyssia. Nothing!

I didn't want to bring my baby into an empty flat with no heating and only the bare floorboards to lie on. I couldn't count on a grant from social services, they'd turned me down the last time, and even though I had Alyssia now, I still wasn't entitled to a budgeting loan or a crisis loan or a maternity grant, because I wasn't receiving the right kind of benefit. Jobseeker's Allowance and income support were qualifying benefits and women who were receiving those could get grants and loans to furnish and decorate their flats. But I was on incapacity benefit because I was in counselling and because of my depression, and that wasn't a qualifying benefit. So I was entitled to nothing.

Such were the vagaries of the system.

I decided to write to one of the big department stores. I explained my circumstances and asked if they had any old display furniture they didn't want. It was a bit presumptuous, I know, but I had nothing to lose – and I had to do something. I'd seen girls leaving hostels unprepared before. They'd only be gone a couple of months and then they'd be back again. It was a cycle of failure and despair. The girls would come in and be given guidance, but most of them didn't use the support constructively and failed to see the significance of it. They didn't fully understand what living independently meant: that they'd have to buy furniture and pay bills and sort out their own hot water and heating. Those things wouldn't be provided automatically, like in the hostels. When they moved out, they weren't properly prepared and ended up having to come back again. I was no exception. When I moved out of the women's refuge and into Noel Road, I didn't know what I was doing. This time it had to be different.

I got a letter back from the department store saying they couldn't give me anything, but they told me about a book called *Grants for Individuals in Need* that I could get from the local library. It was in the reference section and I went there with Alyssia and stayed for four hours, writing down and photocopying all the information I needed. I spent the next three weeks sending individual letters to charities that helped single mothers in my situation. I told them how I came to be here in the first place and my plans for the future – how I wanted to become a functioning member of mainstream society again. Nobody at the unit believed in what I was doing and some even made fun of me for doing it. I waited for a long time without receiving a single reply and I thought it had all been a waste of time and everybody else was right and I was wrong. Then one charity wrote back and said I was eligible for a £200 grant for furniture. They enclosed a cheque that could be processed by the support workers at the unit, who'd have to come with me to make sure I spent the money on what it was intended for, and not on drink or drugs.

Shortly after that, another reply came. Then another. And another. I was able to buy a cooker and a washing machine and beds and a second-hand sofa. One of the charities sent vouchers for a baby store and I went there and bought stuff for Alyssia – sheets and blankets and bottles and nappies and a couple of soft toys. I couldn't believe the generosity of the organizations and the help those wonderful people gave me and I'll be for ever in their debt. Suddenly, all the worries I had about moving out of the unit had dissipated and I was actually looking forward to the future with my daughter. I didn't have much money, but I knew we'd have the basics and that's all we needed to live safe and happy. I'd been so scared it would be like Noel Road – cold and callous, with no food or furniture. But the charities took all that worry away. I just needed to make sure I spent the little money I had on essentials. These things may seem so simple and elemental to most people, but to me back then they were the difference between success and failure, hopelessness and happiness.

I wrote back to all the charities and thanked them for their kindness and consideration. Without them, my life and Alyssia's would have been so much harder. I gave all the information I'd gleaned at the library over to the support workers so they'd be able to advise other girls who came into the unit after me. I have to say here that I have a lot of respect for most of the people who run women's refuges and hostels, and I always hoped someday I could repay them for helping me when I had no one else. It must be so rewarding to be there for someone who's vulnerable and troubled, to help them overcome their difficulties and believe in themselves again. I would love to be able to help others as I was helped. Now, thanks to them, I was ready to go back out into the big blustering world.

All I needed was a place to live.

Then I received a letter from the council saying they were pleased to offer me a two-bedroom flat in the Weoley Castle area of Birmingham. I couldn't wait to go there to take a look at it. I'd never heard of Weoley Castle, even though I'd been round most of Birmingham with Marco in his van, so I wasn't sure what to expect. The council arranged a date for me to view the property and I went down there with Alyssia and one of the support workers. The flat was on the seventh floor of a tower block and we were met by a housing officer. There was a smoky smell of urine all the way up in the lift. The door opposite on my landing was open and a man wearing a wife-beater vest was standing just inside, drinking a can of extra-strong lager. There were three big Alsatian dogs behind him in the hall. They growled at us as we let ourselves into the flat.

They'd told me the flat needed some work doing to it and I expected it was nothing a nice coat of paint wouldn't fix. What they should have said was the place needed burning to the ground! All the windows were either smashed or missing completely. The walls were graffitied from floor to ceiling and the whole place stank like it had been used as a squat or a drug den or a medieval muck-hole. There was nothing in the kitchen, and I mean nothing – not even a sink. A substance that looked like blood was spurted up the walls in the bathroom and the toilet was ready to walk out the door on its own. I was stunned. It was surreal. A nightmare from a dystopian novel. And, according to housing regulations, this was my one and only choice. If I didn't accept this flat, I'd find myself dropped from the register like Alice was. I'd be homeless and on the street again, and they'd probably take Alyssia away from me and put her into care. But how could she live here?

We went back down to the porter's office on the ground floor and the housing officer asked me to sign the forms of acceptance for the flat.

'No.'

'No?'

'I can't bring my baby to live in this place.'

'You don't have a choice.'

'Yes I do!'

When I got back to the mother and baby unit, the support worker who'd come with me confirmed that the flat was uninhabitable and a definite health hazard. But the housing association told me I'd still have to leave the unit as I'd come to the end of my time there and the notice to quit would remain in force. The staff were sympathetic and supported me – I was on good terms with them and even gave them banking and mortgage advice from time to time. But there wasn't much they could do, except allow me to telephone the council's housing department.

'And what's your reason for turning down the flat?'

'It's not fit for rats to live in.'

'That's not a valid reason. We'll be dropping you from the homeless list.'

There was no way, while I had breath in my body, I was going to drag Alyssia round the streets of Birmingham with nowhere to live. I had flashbacks of what it was like before and it frightened me. I had to take on this fight. And I had to win it. As I said, I got on well with the support staff and they let me use their computer to write letters. And I did! I wrote to everyone I could think of: my MP and my doctor and my counsellor, and a six-page letter of complaint to the Directorate of Housing for Birmingham City Council. I submitted my appeal and waited for a reply. I didn't have much time as the notice to quit the mother and baby unit had expired, but I refused to leave and the housing association were taking me to court to get a warrant for bailiffs to enter my flat and reclaim it. I eventually received a letter of apology from the council, along with confirmation that my homeless status was reinstated and I'd be offered an alternative place as soon as one became available. But the clock was ticking. I only had a few weeks left till the bailiffs came banging on my door. So I waited.

And waited.

And waited.

The day before the bailiffs were due, I got a letter offering me a two-bedroom maisonette in Thirlmere Drive, Moseley, and a viewing had been arranged for that very day. There was little time to spare. I was very nervous when I went to see the place – I knew I couldn't turn this down or I'd be on the streets with Alyssia the next day. It was sunny and the street was lined with apple trees. There were bungalows along one side with neatly kept gardens and trimmed hedges. I made my way to the top of the drive and found the block of maisonettes on the right. It looked nice – not a tower block like at Weoley Castle – and there was grass and shrubs outside the front and rows of little gardens round the back. I climbed the stairs to the first floor with Alyssia in my arms and down along the walkway to the front door. The balcony looked out over Moseley Bog Nature Reserve and I remember the colours of the flowers and plants and trees, and the distant floating sound of children playing. I was in love with the place and I hadn't even been inside yet.

The maisonette itself was purpose built and there were six blocks down one side of the drive, which was a cul-de-sac with no through traffic. My block had two two-bedroom flats underneath and four two-bedroom maisonettes on the first floor. The balcony at the rear of the building led to all the front doors and mine was down the very end. Each flat had its own little garden and mine was directly underneath the balcony. Out beyond the houses was the green forest of Moseley Bog, full of wildlife. The sound of birds singing would be the first thing

I'd hear in the mornings. There was a Catholic primary school beside the nature reserve, where Alyssia would go when she was old enough.

Perfect!

The front door opened into a hall, with a large kitchen on the left. Stairs led up to the two bedrooms and bathroom and, on the right, the front room with its huge sunny windows looking out over the street. It was just what I wanted. Secluded. Safe. I knew we'd be happy here and I accepted it straight away.

I arranged for all the goods I'd got from the charities to be delivered on the day I moved in. But I did have some baby stuff, clothes and toys and things, that I had to bring with me. The mother and baby unit arranged for a man with a van to come and collect everything and take me and Alyssia round to Thirlmere Drive. I didn't have much, but it was too much for me to take by myself and manage a baby as well. I was in the back of the van helping the guy load the stuff when he came up behind me and put his hands round my waist. It scared the wits out of me and I was wary of him all the way to the maisonette. He moved the bits and pieces in for me while I looked after Alyssia, but then I couldn't get him to leave.

'You need to go.'

'What about a cup of tea?'

'There's nothing unpacked.'

'Come on . . .'

'Please leave!'

But he wouldn't and I was afraid for Alyssia. I phoned the mother and baby unit and they sent round a support worker and, when she threatened him with the police, he finally left with a scowling finger-sign.

'Slag!'

But it was another scary experience and I've been cautious ever since of finding myself alone with men I don't know. In all I've encountered and learned, I'm aware that it's very easy to give some men the wrong impression – if you act friendly or talk to them or smile or even glance their way, they take it to mean you're interested in them sexually. I don't want to sound paranoid or a prude, but I've had so many bad experiences and near misses that now I'm nervous of being on my own with blokes. You could say it's my own fault: I used the power of physical attraction when it suited me and I don't like it when it doesn't suit me. And that's right, I did. And I was lucky. If something really bad had happened to me back then, I would have accepted it as getting what I deserved. But in my own flat with my daughter, or minding my own business on the street, or in other innocent, everyday situations, I don't think I deserve to be considered easy meat for any man whose ego is telling him that he can get away with being aggressively lecherous.

I lived the life of a recluse when I first moved into the maisonette. I'd been through a lot and I didn't want to expose my emotional side to anyone. I didn't have any friends and I didn't talk to anyone in Thirlmere Drive. The flat had storage heaters instead of central heating and metal window frames and, in winter, the wind whistled through and it was expensive to keep the heaters running.

I complained to the electricity company, but they didn't listen and it took me a long time to get it sorted out. I did in the end, through perseverance and not giving up. Money-wise, it was a hard time. I tended to buy the food my daughter needed first and supermarket brand specials after that. Six tins of white label beans for a pound. Sausages made from cereal boxes. Stuff nearing sell-by date that was reduced in price. I lost a lot of weight and went down to a size eight, the smallest I'd ever been. I did all the work in the maisonette – laying carpets and wallpapering and plumbing in the washing machine. I couldn't afford to pay tradesmen to do anything, so I learned fast how to do everything for myself. I spent two months painting Alyssia's bedroom like it was at the unit, with green carpet like grass and a woodland vista round all the walls, which I painted with little tester pots I took from a big hardware store. It looked like a wonderland in there for her – and she was my enchanted princess.

I spent most of my time decorating the maisonette and taking Alyssia for days out whenever I could afford it. She loved animals and I'd take her to the nature reserve and to city farms, to the sea life centre and zoos. I'd get a day bus pass when I had a bit of money to spare and we'd go all over the place. She loved every minute of it and we were in our own little world. In between the outings, I'd stay in the maisonette. I shopped once every ten days. I'd go out and buy food and other essential things we needed and then I'd just stay in until I had to go shopping again or until I could afford an outing.

Then reality intruded on our idyll. I woke at about 2.00 a.m. one morning feeling really ill. I was vomiting non-stop, to the point where I couldn't breathe properly, and my eyes were streaming. I felt weak and dizzy. Alyssia woke and was crying when she saw me so sick. I tried to comfort her but it was hard because, just when I'd get her calmed down, I'd start throwing up again. My vision began to blur and I felt really frightened. I lived alone and had no contact with anyone around me. If I collapsed on the floor my daughter would have no one to help her. No one would know and she'd be left crying, just as I was in the dark house when I was three. I didn't know how much longer I could stay upright. My legs felt weak and I thought I might pass out at any minute. I called an ambulance.

When the paramedics arrived and realized I was on my own with a small child, they agreed that it would be better for me to go to A&E and they took us both to the hospital. I spent all night there, sleeping on and off in a corridor with Alyssia in my arms. When I was finally examined, they told me I had gastroenteritis and I was put on a drip for dehydration. They let me go later in the day and gave me anti-sickness drugs and some Dioralyte to replace the salts and minerals in my body. But I didn't have enough money to get all the way home. I got a bus as close as I could and then walked the rest of the way, carrying Alyssia. Gastroenteritis is very contagious and, by now, Alyssia had it as well. We both had to go straight to bed when we got home and I wasn't able to eat anything for several days. The anti-sickness medicine stopped the vomiting, but I was very weak for a long time afterwards due to not eating. Alyssia was sick a couple of times and had diarrhoea, but she didn't get it as badly as me, thank goodness. My stomach felt like it had been turned inside out but, without the medicine, I probably would have ended up back in hospital.

Afterwards, when we recovered, I realized it was selfish of me to keep us cocooned in our own little world. I couldn't live like this for the rest of my life. It was a warning and it frightened me. What if something really bad happened? Who would look after Alyssia? When I didn't have a child, I could take stupid chances and put up with the consequences of my irresponsible actions – but now I had another little life to take care of. I was trying to make a perfect world for my daughter, so she wouldn't come into contact with anything bad or dangerous. The irony was, the danger was being created by the very thing I was trying to achieve. I realized what I was doing was futile. The world wasn't a perfect place and, like it or not, she'd have to grow up and find her own space in it. She was going to come into contact with other people, good and bad, just as I had. Some would try to use her, and I couldn't stop that happening. All I could do was be there to pick her up if she fell.

It was summer of 2004 and strange things began to happen round about that time. Optical illusions, tricks of the light. Spectres from the back of my mind. Walking down the street – shopping – I heard familiar voices. Everywhere. I kept seeing things that reminded me of my family. There was a photography shop in King's Heath with a picture in the window that looked just like Nan when she was younger. It was an advertisement for photo restoration, but it stopped me in my tracks when I first walked past it and I kept going back to look again. Then

I saw a man in a lumberjack shirt strolling in the market — a shirt exactly like the one my father used to wear. I walked behind him for a while but he didn't turn round. Names would scroll up in the credits of television programmes — 'Eileen' and 'Harry' — and they'd stare at me from the screen. Once, when I was at a crossroads, I could've sworn I saw them both down at the end of the street. They waved and I waved back and then they were gone. And other things, lots of other little things, kept drawing me back to them. I was sure it was all just coincidence or an aftermath of the illness. I told myself these things happened all the time and normally I wouldn't have even noticed, but being sick had set my mind in motion and I was thinking about family because there was no one else to think about.

Then another letter came from the Salvation Army. It was exactly the same as the one I'd received before. It came via the Department for Work and Pensions again. The Salvation Army had sent them the letter, to go to the person with that particular National Insurance number. The Salvation Army didn't know my address and the DWP weren't allowed to give it to them. All they could do was forward the letter to me. When I got the first letter, I felt grief and anger, a mixture of guilt and hurt and frustration. It accused me of something intangible and that's why I tore it up. It seemed then that I couldn't get rid of my past, even though I wanted to. It kept coming after me, following me, stalking me.

But this time it was different. Many things had changed since that last letter. I was no longer so emotionally unstable; I'd come through counselling and had taken myself apart and rebuilt a new me during that process. I'd examined all my thoughts and feelings about the past. I'd faced them and, although I still felt insecure, it wasn't as bad as before. I was calmer and more in control. Alyssia had had a dramatic effect on my emotions as well. I was happy in a way I'd never known before and the ice in my heart had been thawed by real, real love.

I looked at the letter in my hand with an open mind. I thought about what it would mean to myself and my daughter. But I didn't run to the phone. I put the letter to one side – somewhere safe. Out of sight but not out of mind.

For the future.

17
Cancer

Heaven and hell are just different points of the same view, aren't they? And sometimes it can seem like you're living your life backwards. One day I was walking along the street, feeling fine. A bus drove past me with a sign underneath the back window – 'What's pants, but could save your life?' and it was an NHS advert for women to have cervical screening.

I thought it wouldn't do any harm to have a check, now that I was a mother. There was no reason to think the smear test would come back anything but normal. So I went, and they told me I'd have the results within eight weeks. Ten days later I received a letter telling me the cells that were taken showed signs of an abnormality called 'severe dyskaryosis' and it would need further investigation. I'd need to go to a colposcopy clinic to have my cervix examined. The appointment was made for a week later. At this point, I wasn't too worried: at the bottom of the letter it said only 10 per cent of abnormalities grew into cancer and I might just have to have some laser treatment to my cervix to remove the abnormal cells.

When I went to the colposcopy clinic, I was greeted by the registrar who was going to do whatever it was that had to be done, along with three nurses and a student. I had to remove my clothes from the waist down and lie on a mechanical bed with a cut-out area for my pelvis and my legs up in stirrups. I was raised up to eye level and it was über embarrassing. There is no dignity in a position like that, with everybody peeping and probing. A high-powered microscope was used to scan the surface of my cervix, with the images projected on to a screen next to me on the bed. It all looked fine, like a pink doughnut, to my unclinical eye. The registrar said she'd be applying a vinegar solution and the abnormalities would come up like white grains of rice. They would then use a laser to remove the tiny white spots which were the abnormal cells. Simple, eh?

I watched the screen as they applied the solution and was dismayed to see my whole cervix turn white – there was no pink left. The registrar looked shocked and so did the nurses. The student only looked bemused because she didn't know what she was actually seeing. I turned to the registrar.

'Why has it all gone white?'

'I need to discuss it with the consultant.'

'Is it normal?'

'I'll be back in a minute.'

Obviously, it wasn't normal. So, I was left lying half naked and unable to move, with a camera stuck up me. The nurses tried to make smiling small talk.

'Have you come a long way?'

'What does it mean?'

'The consultant will be here soon.'

After five minutes that seemed like five hours to me, the consultant came bowling into the examination room and took up a position in front of the camera. He applied more vinegar solution and a tiny little brush to take off some of the cells. On the screen, it looked like a toilet brush and at this point my cervix began to bleed. Other people were coming into the room now to have a look at the abnormality and musing speculatively to themselves.

Eventually, the consultant poked his 'hmmmm-ing' head up and looked at me – a serious frown on his face.

'It's vitally important that you come in and have a biopsy done as soon as possible.'

'What's wrong?'

'You'll need to have a general anaesthetic.'

'What's wrong?'

'The whole area needs to be removed –'

'What's wrong?'

'– and sent to the lab for assessment.'

By this time I was really not liking everybody staring up my vagina and I just wanted to get off the bed.

'Can I get off the bed?'

'I don't think you understand the seriousness of this.'

'Tell me, then!'

'You have to come in and have this procedure done.'

'Why can't you do it now?'

'You need a general anaesthetic.'

Nobody said the word 'cancer', but everybody was thinking it, including me. A million things were running through my head. Who'll look after my daughter while I'm having the operation? How long will it take? Will it hurt? What were all the white cells? When will they tell me what's wrong? The hospital people were all conversing with each other in medi-speak while I got dressed and I wanted to run out of the room and pretend I'd never come in for the smear test in the first place. Before I was able to do so, the consultant took me to one side.

'At this point we can't be specific.'

'Why can't you?'

'We don't know the level of the abnormality.'

'Why not?'

'We can't just remove a sample, the whole area needs to be tested.'

He still didn't tell me what all the white stuff meant, or what kind of abnormality I had and he booked me in for the operation in two weeks' time.

I was thinking, 'This is bad that they want me back so fast,' while they droned on like white noise in the background about it being a cone biopsy using Leetz, a fine piece of wire with an electrical current running through it which would cut a loop of tissue out of my cervix. If I had been listening, I would have grimaced. I had to say the word.

'Is it cancer?'

'We don't know yet.'

'What are the chances?'

'That it is or isn't?'

'That it is!'

'Chances are it isn't.'

How could this be happening? I only came in for a check-up to begin with and now this! I was healthy. I had no symptoms of any sort. No pains. No lumps. This must all be some big mistake. But I saw it on camera – the whiteness. I saw it with my own eyes and every part was white, so every part must be contaminated – abnormal – gone bad. A part of my body had gone bad and had to be removed.

It was no more than I deserved for the things I'd done. But my little daughter had done nothing wrong, so why punish her for my sins? And how could the doctors not know? They were doctors, they should know, they were paid to know! They gave me a pile of leaflets that were meant to explain everything, but I couldn't read them. All the words and images blurred and swam over the pages when I tried. I just wanted to go home and hug Alyssia. I didn't sleep well that night. When I'd gone in for the colposcopy that morning, they'd assured me it was just a safety precaution, routine, and I had nothing to worry about. But then I saw the reactions of the staff while they were looking at my cervix and the sudden frowns and the hushed tones and the running off to get the consultant. That wasn't routine at all. When I went in I was at ease. When I came out I was in shock. It felt as if my body was turning against me and I couldn't help wondering if it was something I'd done that caused this. Was it a penance for walking out and leaving my family with all that worry? Or was it because of the dissolute life I'd led since doing that? Cancer! It seemed such an extreme price to have to pay.

People died of cancer – didn't they?

Next morning, I did the worst thing possible: I took Alyssia down to the library and I Googled what was on the leaflets. What a mistake! Cervical Intraepithelial Neoplasia 1 and CIN2 and CIN3 and severe dyskariosis and biopsy and bleeding and colposcopy and carcinoma and cancer – I was freaking out by the time I finished. What if it was cancer? Of course it was cancer! What if I died? Who would look after my daughter? She'd be taken into care and abused and end up like one of the girls at the refuge. No! I read through the leaflets – over and over – and I kept coming up with the only solution – the one I didn't want.

But I was jumping the gun – crossing the bridge before I came to it – trying to put the fire out before it caught light. I needed to calm down or I'd go crazy. Again. Alyssia needed me to be composed, not neurotic. All the old feelings were coming back – helplessness, despair, paranoia, depression, panic – and I couldn't allow them to take hold of me again.

When I left the mother and baby unit, I'd been allocated an outreach support worker and she took Alyssia for the day, even though I didn't want to leave her, but I had no other option. I was admitted to hospital at 7.30 a.m. The surgery was fairly routine and went without any problems. I woke up around noon and was desperate to get out and see my little girl. They told me they'd removed about three centimetres of cervical tissue and it would be sent for analysis. If cancer was found, I'd be called back within two weeks. If the tests were negative, I'd get the results in six weeks. They asked me to fill some papers out, which I did without reading them, then I left. I was very hungry from fasting but I couldn't eat anything. I looked pale and drawn from the worry, and was dizzy and bleeding by the time I got home.

The waiting was the worst part. It was unbearable. I lost a stone in weight as the days turned into weeks – one into two into three into four. Five weeks went past and I was gradually becoming more relaxed because I hadn't heard anything. I was starting to allow myself to believe the biopsy tests were negative and I'd get the results soon. I still hadn't heard anything after six weeks, so I called the colposcopy clinic to find out why.

'The doctors are all in a meeting.'

'I just need the results of my biopsy tests.'

'That's what they're discussing.'

The nurses couldn't tell me anything. They said a letter would be sent to me. I waited, but no letter came. I started ringing every day, trying to talk to someone, anyone, who could tell me what was happening.

Finally, a Macmillan Cancer Support nurse called me back and my heart sank. She spoke at length and in plain English about why my results were taking so long. The doctors had to have a multidisciplinary meeting because of the high level of infection and it took time to get them all together – or something like that. I believed there was a bit of covering up going on and somebody should have been in contact with me long before then. But the news wasn't good.

I did have cancer.

But, as far as she knew, it had all been removed with the biopsy and there might be nothing to worry about. I received a letter the next day saying invasive cancer cells had been found in the biopsy and I needed to come in in two days' time to see the consultant again. My worst fears had come true, but maybe they'd removed it like the Macmillan nurse had said. Somehow, though, it felt like I wasn't being told everything, as if they were keeping something back, being conspiratorial. I went in to see the consultant and I was feeling anxious, to say the least. He smiled condescendingly.

'We'd like you to have a second operation.'

'Why?'

'We found invasive cancer cells in the biopsy.'

'I was told you'd removed the cancer.'

Apparently, it was an aggressive strain that had grown quickly and, yes, they believed they'd removed all the affected cells with the biopsy.

'You believe?'

'Because of the number of affected cells, we feel it prudent you should have a second biopsy, just to be on the safe side.'

'Do I or do I not have cancer?'

'You had cancer, but we've removed it.'

'As far as you know.'

'We would prefer to err on the side of caution. I would strongly advise a second procedure.'

'Can't I just have a hysterectomy?'

He explained that I was too young for a hysterectomy and they would only consider it as a last resort.

The second biopsy was arranged for 22 August, my daughter's birthday. I'd planned to take Alyssia out for the day to celebrate, so now we had to celebrate the day before. I didn't try to explain why. We had cake and presents, and I took her to Drayton Manor Theme Park, where we spent the day on the rides. I wanted to do normal things, to forget about the cancer cells for one day. I wanted to spend time with my daughter, without her having a care in the world, and for us to have some fun – just for one day, before reality came back to haunt me. I also wanted to give my daughter a day I hoped she'd remember with me, in case the worst came to the worst. In case the unthinkable became thinkable. Again.

The second operation wasn't as routine as the first. I woke feeling really groggy and in pain. The bed sheets and my legs were covered in blood and my stomach hurt really badly. I felt out of it, not really conscious, and I looked like I'd been run over by an articulated lorry. I tried to get up to leave, just like I did the first time, but I collapsed back on to the bed. A nurse came to clean me up and it took another couple of hours for me to get myself back together. A doctor came round to see me.

'It was a large loop biopsy this time. We wanted to make sure we didn't leave anything behind.'

'Did you leave any cervix behind?'

He smiled.

'About one centimetre.'

I was discharged later that day, after some more clinical exposition that was devoid of emotion or compassion, and I had to go through the waiting game again. I started getting really bad pain in the area that had been operated on, I had a fever and felt absolutely vile. I still had to look after Alyssia, so I couldn't really be sick, and I was put on a course of antibiotics. After a week, I was still sick and bleeding more than ever, so they put me on Metronidazole, the strongest antibiotic available. I had an allergic reaction and had to be rushed to hospital at four in the morning. It felt like my head was going to explode, I couldn't see straight and I was vomiting non-stop. They wanted me to stay in and rest, but I had a child to take care of who was being looked after by someone I didn't really know, although I did trust her – I had to trust her. They let me back out the next day, but told me I couldn't lift anything or carry anything, including my daughter, and I should get as much rest as possible.

Eight weeks went by and I hadn't received the results of the second biopsy and was still having irregular bleeding. I was given another colposcopy appointment. I knew what to expect this time – naked from the waist down and back on the sadistic voyeuristic bed. They found that the wound from the second operation hadn't healed and was seeping. I was treated there and then, and given another course of antibiotics.

Due to the strength of the medicine, I got thrush throughout my whole body – everywhere! It was in my mouth and my vagina, at the backs of my knees, under my breasts and in my armpits, and I was itching and flaking and blistering and burning as if I was in the seventh circle of hell. Another side effect caused me to be violently sick if I went out in sunlight. But I healed, eventually, and I finally got the biopsy results after another six weeks, saying that all the cancerous cells had successfully been removed and I just had to come in and be checked every six months. The only lasting effect was the amount of weight I'd lost and how weak I felt. But I was going to live to be with my daughter and that's all that mattered to me.

I started to breathe again.

Six months later, just before I was due back for my first check-up, the irregular bleeding came back, but I didn't tell anyone because I couldn't deal with the antibiotics again. The check-up tests were comprehensive, to say the least: colposcopy, blood and vaginal ultrasound and hysteroscopy. Now, a hysteroscopy is a thing like a kebab skewer with a camera on the end of it and it's inserted into the cervix to examine the interior of the uterus to see what's going on with the endometrial lining and the ovaries. However, what was left of my cervix was little more than scar tissue and extremely tight and, when they tried to insert this thing, I kicked the doctor in the face. They should never have done it without anaesthetic. It was probably the most painful experience of my entire life and I ended up with a facial twitch below my right eye for two weeks. The hysteroscopy revealed no problems, but the vaginal ultrasound showed I had polycystic ovary syndrome, where blood-filled cysts grow on the ovaries and eventually pop, causing pain and irregular bleeding and sending my hormones crazy. They offered me a hormonal coil to try to remedy it, but I declined. I'd had enough things shoved up me for now.

Other than that, I was fine!

The worst part of the whole thing was worrying about my daughter. In the hospital, the nurses had this patronizing look of pity on their faces, like I was some sort of child. But the way I looked at it, there was something inside me I had to fight. There really wasn't anything else on my mind. I didn't have the option of getting ill. I didn't feel sorry for myself or sad, I just felt like I was going to fight and fight and fight until I got that bad thing out of my body. It was my job to raise my daughter. She didn't ask to be brought into the world, and I had no intention of leaving this earth before that job was done.

When I was going through all this, it made me think back to when I'd tried to kill myself and I realized how lucky I was not to have succeeded. Now I wanted to live so much. I suppose it was a kind of payback time – I was being shown what it's really like to have your life on the line and how stupid I'd been to even think about ending it. I'd finally realized how precious life is. No matter how bad things got in the future, I would never consider suicide as an option again.

We're so lucky to have each day we live – each hug and heartache, each smile and sigh, each thrill and tear.

18
Family

I took the Salvation Army letter from its hiding place and looked at it again.

When I first held Alyssia in my arms, I instantly knew I would love her for ever and I would be there for her always. And now I thought about what it would be like to lose her. That's when I first allowed myself to imagine how Nan and my father felt when I went missing. When I first left, I was convinced they'd hate me for my mistakes, just like I hated myself. But now, because of the love I felt for my little girl, I wondered if that was true. Maybe their love was like mine and it could overlook any mistake, overcome any obstacle, any trauma. Maybe it could accept and understand? I thought about making contact again, and then I had to think about what that would mean. How would they react, even if they did still love me? How would I react, even if I did still love them? I had a conversation with myself, weighing the pros and cons, swaying from one point of view to another, swinging back and forth.

When I left, my life was a shambles with debts everywhere, including the mortgage repayments I'd failed to make. What if they'd lost the house because of me? I swung away from making contact. How could I face them? I'd feel the guilt again, it would close in on me and tear at me. I could see the frowning faces, the pointing fingers, hear the harsh tones of voice. Everything fell apart because of me. I ruined everybody's life when I ran away. But no, it wouldn't be like that. Why were they still trying to contact me if they felt like that? I swung back to the idea of getting in touch. And I missed them, more so now I had Alyssia. It wasn't just that I needed them to be there in case the cancer came back; I wanted Alyssia to have a family, to know her family. But what about the debts? Would they still be there to drag me back down? What about people I knew, friends of the family, neighbours, people I'd worked with – what would they think of me if I came back after my meltdown? I'd have to face them all – sooner or later. A lump developed in my throat and swelled until it almost choked me. Panic. Heartbeat. I felt like running again. And I probably would have, if I hadn't had Alyssia.

I put the letter away, but I couldn't get it out of my mind. I thought maybe I should tear it up, like I did with the first one. But I just couldn't bring myself to do it. Thoughts came to me in my sleep – or what passed for sleep sometimes. They crept in through my ear and whispered to my unsuspecting brain: 'Do it, Shelley! Shelley! Shelley!' The sound of my name being called seemed to echo through my brain, getting smaller and further away all the time. Then it came back loud, like someone was standing beside the bed, and I'd wake. When I left London I'd been able to suppress all my feelings, making myself numb and cold. I pushed all my emotions away until there was nothing left inside me but that big hole full of ice. But the counselling and the birth of my daughter brought those feelings back again – and they weren't all bad like I thought they would be. They didn't destroy me like I expected them to.

I went to find the letter again.

But, before I got to it, I thought about all the questions I'd have to face. Where were you? What were you doing? How did you survive? I didn't relish telling people how I'd survived. I wasn't proud of it. Then there'd be more questions. How could you do it? Didn't you care? That's what I would have asked – perfectly legitimate questions. So I walked away and left the letter where it was. Was I a bad person? Was I? I didn't do it to hurt anyone. I did it because I couldn't cope any longer, because something snapped in my head and the survival instinct took over. Fight or flight. And I knew I couldn't fight it. Would they think I was mad? I thought I was back then – or that I was going mad. I was certainly acting crazy before I left.

I was a new person now, free of that hysterical history. Surely it would be better to leave things as they were? I looked at Alyssia and I knew these conversations with myself were all going to be irrelevant. I didn't care about money any more, or having the latest TV, the best phone. I smiled when I saw the sun, when blossom from the trees drifted down on to me as I passed underneath. I was filled with something I could only call joy when I heard my daughter's laugh, and when we hugged I was beyond the badness in the world and nothing else mattered. Nothing. And I felt strong.

But maybe not strong enough to beat the cancer, if it came back. I recited the litany of small reasons why I shouldn't make contact – and the big reason why I should. It was only a matter of time till the inevitable moment arrived.

I left the letter for another few days, but I was drifting towards it, getting closer to it. I told myself I needed to be absolutely certain. No more mistakes. One thing I decided, I didn't want to move back to London. It would overpower me. I had to stay in Birmingham, at least for another while. I was a new person now and I knew I wouldn't fit back into the old life. Things could never be the same as before. And what about Alyssia – what would they think? That one was easy. I didn't care what they'd think. I had no pressure in my life now, apart from the fear of the cancer coming back, and that over-ruled everything. I couldn't take a chance. I couldn't gamble with Alyssia's future. She had to know her family in case anything happened to me. She had no father – he'd chosen to not be part of her life. She had no brothers or sisters and never would have. But she had a great-nan and a granddad and uncles and aunts, and I didn't have the right to keep her from them. If I did that I'd be no better than Marco, no different to my mother – unfair and unfeeling.

I'd already made my decision. I was just postponing the inevitable action. Mentally, I'd decided, but I still had to get up and physically do it. Which was more difficult. I held back from the letter because the one thing I wasn't prepared to do was go back to being the woman I was before.

I would not make those mistakes again. I was in control of my life now, apart from the cancer, and it was going to stay like that. I'd worked so hard to detach myself – been through so much – and this one phone call could change everything. I was no longer that Mackenney girl who left London, stumbling around trying to find herself in a dark and disordered place – trying to find somewhere to fit in. I'd learned a lot and knew who I was at last. I was stronger and able to face my failings, my faults and insecurities. This is what I believed.

I decided to speak to the Salvation Army first, to find out exactly what my family had said to them. I got the letter and opened it.

Then I dialled, withholding my number in case things went wrong.

It took me a century to press each button on the phone. My finger moved in slow motion and the dialling sound was deafening. Then I waited an eternity for someone to answer. I was going to hang up several times and my heart was beating faster than the wings of a hummingbird – *ring ring* – beat beat – *ring ring* – beat beat – *ring ring* – beat beat. My stomach was churning and my mouth was dry – *ring ring* – beat – when a man's voice finally answered.

'Salvation Army.'

The voice was emotionless and clinical. Metallic. I tried to speak in reply, but no words came.

'Hello . . .'

Nothing.

'Hello!'

Eventually –

'I'm Shelley Mackenney.'

'Yes?'

'You sent me a letter.'

Within seconds, his tone changed completely. He was suddenly gushing, ecstatic, overwhelmed. I tried to stay as cool as I could, but I knew my voice was sounding strained.

'I need to ask you some questions.'

'By all means. Please do.'

I asked if my family was still looking for me or if the second letter was something that was computer generated and sent out periodically.

'Yes, your family is still trying to trace you, Shelley.'

I asked why they were still looking for me.

'Because they love you and are worried about you.'

I made it clear to him that this was just a preliminary call and I might not take it any further.

'Of course, Shelley. That's your prerogative.'

Then the crucial question. I asked where my family was living now. I needed to know if they'd lost the house because I ran away. If that had happened, then I would have hung up the phone.

'Forty-nine Crutchley Road, Downham, London.'

I breathed such a sigh of relief.

I think the man could sense how nervous I was, even though I was doing my very best to sound controlled. He told me he was a colonel in the Salvation Army and my call would be treated in the strictest of confidence. He said I didn't have to contact them, but my father and grandmother would be really happy to hear from me. If I liked, he could call them and tell them I'd been in touch, just to put their minds at ease and give me time to prepare myself in case I wanted to take things further. He could pre-arrange a time for me to call, so they'd be expecting it and it wouldn't come out of the blue.

'No!'

'No?'

'If I'm going to ring them, it has to be now.'

'Very well, if that's what you'd prefer.'

The colonel was extremely diplomatic, careful, cautious, trying not to spook me like a frightened fawn. Adrenaline was pumping through my body. I was sitting on a chair and I couldn't keep my legs still – they were bouncing up and down on arched toes. My voice was faster and more high-pitched than usual, and it took every ounce of willpower to resist the flight instinct that was screaming at me to slam down the phone. He gave me the number. It was the same as it was when I ran away, but I didn't recognize it. If I called now, without any warning, I'd be able to tell from the tone of their voices if they were really happy to hear from me, or if they were angry. Hospitable or hostile.

It had to be now.

Or never.

After talking to the Salvation Army, I sat with the phone for three hours – picking it up, putting it down and picking it up again. I tried over and over to dial the number, but couldn't bring myself to. Every time I thought 'this is it', some fear would come into my mind and I'd put the phone down again. I lit cigarette after cigarette. It's hard to explain how difficult this was to do. Over and over again I said to myself, 'I'm going to do it now,' but I'd back off because the words I planned to say dried up in my mouth and evaporated. I got up and paced the room. My hands were shaking and I was going hyper, like I used to before when I was under severe stress. I had to calm down, get a grip, pull myself together. All the clichés crowded inside my head, scolding me, folding me frantic. The hands of the clock ticked round and I was getting worse and worse. Alyssia was in bed asleep and some audience participation programme on the television was trying to tell me something – all standing up and screaming at me. *Do it! Don't do it!* I turned the set off and sat amongst the silences in the maisonette.

The thoughts began to run faster through my head, so fast I couldn't keep up with them. Faster and faster. Was I going crazy again? Was this close proximity to life in London sending me into mental seizure again? I stood up and put my hands to my head, which was hurting now. I walked round the room in a circle. I went to the kitchen and made myself a cup of coffee and, as I sat there at the table with a kaleidoscope of white noise whirling round me, I had a kind of epiphany. I realized that humanity was only truly observable at arm's length. If you came too close it was a mass of random patterns and abstracts and waves, and, from a distance, it blended into the larger surroundings and was no longer distinguishable from them.

And that was the answer.

I went back into the front room and started to dial the number.

I had my plan. I was ready to make this call. I'd speak to my family, but keep them at arm's length. Because I felt so protective of Alyssia, I had a deeper understanding of their protectiveness towards me. I'd built up my mental defences and covered every scenario in my mind. Nothing was going to take me by surprise here, nothing was going to catch me off guard. All right, I'd have to explain – apologize even – let them know I didn't do it deliberately to hurt anyone. I just hadn't known what else to do at the time. And I felt obliged to let them know I was alive and well and there was no need for them to worry. I hadn't been raped or murdered and wasn't lying dead in a shallow grave somewhere. I wasn't an alcoholic or a drug addict and I had a nice place now and was happy. However, I'd also survived cancer and had a daughter.

Arm's length!

The phone only rings twice before Nan answers it.

'Hello.'

'Hello, Nan.'

'Who's that?'

The pitch of her voice rises and I can feel the sense of nervous surprise coming through the phone.

'It's Shelley.'

I can hardly hear the words. They trickle out of my mouth and evaporate before they even enter the phone. There's a silence on the other end for a moment, but I can hear Nan breathing.

'Is it really you, Shell?'

'It's me.'

'Oh, Shell, where 'ave you been? We've missed you so much. How are you? What 'ave you been doing? Where are you?'

There's a commotion in the background as she shouts to whoever is with her.

''Ere, it's Shelley! Shelley's on the phone!'

She doesn't cry and neither do I, but there are tears between us that are dry and silent and only for ourselves to feel. I can hear the others, all excited, somewhere behind her shouting.

'Shelley!'

'It's Shelley!'

'Shelley's on the blower!'

Then they're trying to get the phone from Nan, but she's not letting go of it and I'm losing it – my cool – forgetting the plan – caught off guard – falling apart. Waiting for the tears that can't come to fall down my face. Then a man's big voice comes on the phone.

'Who is this?'

It's my father and I feel like I'm five years old again.

'It's me, Dad.'

'Is it? Is it you, Shelley?'

'Yes it is.'

'Are you all right?'

'I'm fine, Dad.'

I hear him sigh and his sense of relief comes through to me, even though he says nothing else for a mind-stopping moment. All my new-woman resolve and supposed strength give way and I'm spun round in an emotional maelstrom – but it's diffused with a welcome warmth, not twisted with pain, and I can't speak either. My father comes back.

'Shelley . . . where are you?'

'I'm here, Dad.'

'No, I mean where *are* you?'

They know I'm in Birmingham, so there's no point in lying about it. Anyway, there's been enough lies. I don't want to resume where I left off.

'I'm in Birmingham, Dad.'

I think about arm's length and it's as if my father is able to read my mind.

'It's all right, Shelley. As long as you're OK.'

'Thanks, Dad.'

'No one wants to crowd you or rush you. You've made contact and that's good enough for now.'

'I'll call again tomorrow.'

'That would be great.'

And that was it. I hung up the phone. I'd done it. They didn't ask me to come home and I didn't give them my phone number. Small steps. Arm's length. Maybe they'd learned a few things too. I'd been away from them for a long time and proved I could live on my own, without anyone minding me – shadowing me – watching over me every minute of the day and night. I didn't tell them about the cancer, because that would have panicked them and I didn't tell them about Alyssia, because that would have been too much for them to take in. For now, I needed to let what had just happened sink in. With one phone call, my life had taken a new direction. It didn't threaten who I was, like I thought it would. If anything, it enhanced who I was now.

But I'd done it. I'd made the call and survived it. What was supposed to happen now? I was relieved I'd made contact, but I wasn't ready to jump in the deep end yet. I wasn't in a hurry to rush down to London for a reunion. I knew it was the right decision to ring, but I didn't want anything to upset the little world I had here with Alyssia. I rang again the next day and kept to the arm's-length plan. My family were acting like the Salvation Army colonel – softly, softly – so's not to spook me. We made small talk mostly, about how things were in Catford and what was happening in Downham, and I told them about Birmingham and the jobs I'd had and what my maisonette was like, but nothing bad – nothing about the hostels or being abducted or homeless or hanging around the city centre making cheap money from men. It was all surface stuff, nothing too deep or difficult, and, after a few days, I gave them my number so they could ring me back.

My father called every day to ask me if I was all right. But, after a while, he started to dig a bit deeper. Why did I leave? Why didn't I tell him I was troubled? He wasn't trying to make me feel guilty – he was the one feeling guilty and he was trying to say he was sorry and he would have helped if he'd only known. But everyone had their own troubles at the time and mine went unnoticed. He didn't understand what could have been bad enough to make me just up and leave my life behind. But then, he'd been on the run for a lot of his own life, hadn't he? I tried to explain as best I could without hurting him or Nan, but it was difficult. It upset Nan to hear about it and it upset me to talk about it. So we let it be. Left well enough alone. We let sleeping dogs lie – in case they got up and bit us.

Three weeks went by and then my father asked if he could come up to see me. I was hesitant – everything had been at arm's length until now, but this would be up close, where life was a mass of random patterns and abstracts and waves.

'There's no pressure, Shelley, only if you want me to.'

'I'm not coming back to London, Dad.'

'That's OK, I'm not asking you to.'

So I agreed. I thought I'd be so nervous, frightened even. But I wasn't. I felt excited at the prospect of his visit. I'd been through so much, my emotions were wrung dry and I'd somehow managed to bring a bit of order into my life. I saw the world in a different light now and I knew it had to be like this. I couldn't keep them at arm's length for ever. I decided long ago that I wasn't going to keep moving every time my family caught wind of where I was. My daughter deserved some stability in her life and I wasn't going to drag her from hostel to hostel or from flat to flat. I'd seen all that with Emily and I swore when Alyssia was born it wouldn't be the same for her. There would be no more running.

Or so I thought.

When I was in counselling, I was made to ask myself what I was running from and why I kept running. I believed it was because I couldn't cope with my debts and, although that was the trigger, the catalyst, I discovered I was really running from myself. In times of extreme stress, my defence mechanism was to get away from it all and pretend it wasn't happening. I disassociated myself from what was frightening me. I ran and made out I was someone else and it was all happening to that other person I'd left behind. Once I'd convinced myself of that lie, I didn't feel the depression any more – I wasn't enveloped in the darkness. I was no longer Shelley Mackenney, so I didn't have any of her problems. I was in identity denial.

Although I was never diagnosed as such, the condition was known in medical terms as 'disassociation disorder' or 'dissociative amnesia', where a traumatic event or series of events causes a person to distance themselves from the situation, to get so far away that they no longer feel the pain. They become someone else and are no longer affected by the torment of their previous self. They simply forget who they were and start over as who they are. It seemed to me the definition fitted how I felt at the time. And I was no stranger to that feeling. It had happened to me before – when I was three.

After the night my mother runs away and I'm taken to live with Nan, I leave the little crying girl in the dark house with the locked door and I become someone else. A new person is living a new life at 49 Crutchley Road and I remember the event like an outsider – like I'm watching it from somewhere outside myself. I can see a girl crying, but that girl isn't me. Even at such a young age, I'm disassociating myself from that haunting experience, as if it's happening to someone else. I refuse to acknowledge the hurt I'm experiencing. But the heartache always comes back to follow me and I'm just storing up problems for the future. The person underneath always surfaces. The other girl always comes back!

So, I wasn't really running from my family, I was running because it was in my nature to do so. When I finally realized and understood this, I didn't need to run any more, I just needed to manage the urge to escape. And

that's what I was doing now: resisting the flight impulse –
telling myself there were other options to running.

Like standing my ground.

Facing the music.

19
Nan

I still hadn't told anyone about Alyssia. I don't know why – I was so proud of her. Maybe it was because her father wasn't around and they might think me cheap or stupid for having a child with a man who didn't love either of us enough to stay. How could I possibly explain that it was me who didn't love him – didn't want him to stick around. Maybe I did as a father for Alyssia, but certainly not as a partner for me. I didn't need him and could do it all for myself. But how could I get my family to understand that?

I gave my father my address and spent the days until his arrival cleaning and painting, tidying and trimming, because I didn't want him thinking I was living in a louse-house. He drove up in a big red tail-lift truck that took up most of the street and all the neighbours were rubbernecking and curtain-twitching. I went out to meet him with Alyssia in my arms. He was so tall, just like I remembered, and he had a great big smile. We hugged and he kissed my forehead, and I felt so proud I wanted to shout out to everyone, 'This is my father!'

'Who's this?'

'This is Alyssia, your granddaughter.'

'I'm too young and good-looking to be a grandfather.'

We laughed and went inside.

I made him tea and we talked. It was relaxed and easy, just like the old days in his car, and I felt like I was five again. The memories came bubbling back up inside me: the closeness we'd had during the short little spells of time we spent together and the smell of diesel oil and gym sweat, and all the curves and corners of this man who wasn't mad, but sometimes bad, and definitely dangerous to know. He didn't ask me about Alyssia's father and I didn't ask him about the big red truck outside. I could see he loved his granddaughter by the look in his eyes and that was enough from a man who rarely showed his soul. He inspected the maisonette from top to bottom, like he was making sure there was an escape route in case the police came crashing through the door. He nodded his head several times and that was his seal of approval, so to speak.

He didn't like the term 'granddad' because it gave his age away and he was always a bit on the vain side like that, but Alyssia called him 'man' to begin with, so he was satisfied. We talked for hours and he just wanted to make sure I was really all right and that nothing bad had happened to me, that I wasn't on drugs or been attacked or raped or ravished. He told me the family had managed to keep the house by ducking and diving like they always did – little earners here and there, that kind of thing – to make the mortgage payments. And, because of the way the mortgage was set up in Nan's name, none of my creditors could stake any claim to it either. The creditors themselves were given the bum's rush and when they sent collectors or bailiffs round, they were all run out of the front garden. The debts were in my name and the family weren't liable for them. As far as the moneylender was concerned, apparently someone had a word in his ear – to the effect that he'd be missing a kneecap or an elbow if he didn't go quietly away. My father smiled and said I didn't need to be scared of anything or anybody because everything had been taken care of.

He went back out to the lorry and carried in half a dozen big bags. It was all my clothes and everything I'd left behind in London: boots and shoes, jewellery, perfume and make-up, stuff I never thought I'd see again. And it felt like a little bit of me had come back from obscurity.

There was a kind of emptiness in the flat when he went. He was always a man who left something of himself behind in a room, some essence of himself, some signature that he'd been there. My father was a man loved and hated at the same time, admired and reviled. But always extraordinary, larger than life. He was affectionate and aggressive and charming and churlish, all things to all men – and some women. I felt lost for a few moments, like before, when he'd have to run away and leave me behind. Back then, I didn't know if he'd be coming back or if he was gone for good – like my mother.

But now it was different.

Over the next nine months, my father came up to visit a couple of times more. And every time I was waiting for the inevitable.

'Your nan wants to come see you.'

'It's a long way.'

'Well, as you won't come to London . . .'

And so it was arranged. If I was nervous about seeing

my father for the first time since I'd gone missing, it was nothing to how I felt when I was waiting for Nan to arrive. To understand my anxiety, you would have to know my nan. As I've said before, her book *Borstal Girl* tells her story and it's hard and brutal; she was the toughest woman I've ever known. Nobody messed with Eileen Mackenney and, if you did, you'd live to regret it. Nan said what she thought and told it as it was; she didn't pull her punches and what you got was what you deserved.

I trembled at the thought of her arrival.

I really wanted to show Nan how well I'd come through everything. She'd gone through so much in her own life and never gave up and never backed down and I felt a bit of a fraud compared to her – I'd let my problems escalate to such a degree when they were nothing compared to what she'd endured. But then, her traumas had been mainly physical and mine had been psychological, so I suppose you couldn't compare them, really. The maisonette wasn't a palace or anything, but it was my home now and I wanted her to like it. Her approval still meant mountains to me, even though I tried to tell myself it didn't. No matter how tough and independent I thought I was, Nan was tougher, more independent. They broke the proverbial mould when they made her and threw away the pieces so it could never be put together again.

I spent two days cleaning the place from top to bottom – I mean everything. I washed and wiped and polished and disinfected and, on the day of her arrival, I looked at my net curtains and thought they weren't very white. I went to a local shop with Alyssia in her buggy to buy some curtain whitener, but they didn't have any.

I went to the next shop and the next and the next – I walked for miles. I couldn't stop until I found it. I can only assume it was nerves or something because it became a small obsession. I finally found some and raced back home and emptied the whole lot into the washing machine, throwing the curtains in after it. I must have put too much in because it started to bubble up and spill out through the detergent tray. More and more bubbles came out and floated around the flat as it erupted like a foamy volcano. In the end I had to turn the machine off and drain all the foam out through the filter. I couldn't believe it: the maisonette had no nets and looked like a squat from the outside, while I was on my hands and knees in the kitchen with a bucket under the filter.

Then Nan knocked on the door.

My father is with her and I have foam all over my hands and face when I open the door. I'm hyper and stressed, but I try hard not to show it.

'Dad, Nan . . . come in.'

My father smiles that smile of his and Nan and I stand face to face for the first time since I ran away, since we parted outside that betting shop and she said she'd see me at lunchtime. So long ago. I have to tell you that my grandmother, Eileen Mackenney, is not a huggy, kissy kind of person – regardless of the circumstances. A cup of tea is always her greeting. It's like a peace offering. If you're offered tea, then you're all right, you're in, you're welcome. So we don't hug or kiss.

'I'll put the kettle on.'

I show them into the front room and there's Alyssia,

still asleep in her buggy from the long walk to find the curtain whitener. Nan stops dead in her tracks and looks down at her great-granddaughter. My heart skips a beat. Time freezes. Stands still. Outside, it's rushing past like an express train but, inside the maisonette, it stops altogether and we're in suspended animation. Then Nan's whole face breaks into a rare beam and everything resumes its normal motion. We have tea and talk and Alyssia wakes up and Nan takes her on her lap and the two of them seem to connect. They're talking to each other even though I'm sure neither knows what the other is saying, and has no need to. My father hasn't told her about Alyssia, but she's not completely surprised because she heard a child in the background during some of the phone calls and she kind of guessed I'd had a baby.

We talk on and I show her round the maisonette. I try to explain what happened to me, but she gets a bit upset so I stop. Not upset at me, just upset about it all – maybe she's feeling some guilt, the same as my father. I don't continue. It's all irrelevant now. Instead, I ask her if she'd like to go for a walk and take a look round the area. It's a quiet day and she agrees. By this time I've totally changed my appearance from the way I used to look in London. Back then, I always wore trendy clothes, did my hair and nails, and wore heels and make-up. Now I dress all in black. Baggy combat trousers and T-shirts, a black baseball cap with my hair tucked away and a black parka coat with a heavy hood that I pull up over the baseball cap. I wear trainers instead of heels and never wear make-up any more. I walk with my head down so the brim of my hat covers my eyes. I just want to blend into the background and for no one to recognize or pay any attention to me. It's camouflage and I don't even notice the transformation.

But Nan does.

'Jesus, Shelley, what the bleedin' 'ell you wearing?'

'What?'

'Why are you dressed like a bleedin' moth?'

She means a Goth. I'm not, but it's her interpretation of my outfit. I pull down the hood, take the baseball cap off, shake my hair loose and laugh. She doesn't know what I'm laughing at, but she laughs too.

Nan visited three or four more times before she came to live with me.

It was about a year after her first visit when she decided to come and stay for a while. After our first meeting, we were speaking on the phone every day. For me, it was like finding an old friend again – a best friend. During that twelve months or so, some really bad things were happening in London – and the final straw came when 49 Crutchley Road was raided by the police yet again. I remember Nan being in a state on the phone to me – she'd come back from shopping and there were dozens of riot police waiting. They ransacked the house. It was all escalating and she was getting older and couldn't cope with it any more. My grandmother was a super-strong woman, but the constant harassment and intimidation were getting too much for her.

'The Mackenneys is number one on their list, Shell. They're out to get us.'

'Look, why don't you come stay with me till it blows over?'

'I don't know . . .'

'Just for a short while.'

'I'll think about it.'

The maisonette was on the first floor of the block, but it was like a little house, it had its own garden and the area was quiet and law-abiding.

It took her a month to make up her mind but, finally, the mounting police vendetta and repression drove her out. I don't know if she really wanted to come up to Birmingham or not – probably not, but I feared for her safety.

'Just for a short while, Shell.'

I moved into Alyssia's room and redecorated my bedroom and bought a new bed for her. I wanted to make the place as comfortable as possible because I knew it would be a huge wrench for her to leave southeast London, where she'd lived all her life. And I was right. She found it very difficult to settle into the seclusion, so she went home. Nan was a very wary person from the years of police persecution; she liked to know who was living around her and to talk to people, to find out who was who and what was what. Since moving into Thirlmere Drive, I'd spoken to nobody and knew nothing, so the isolation was difficult for her. She came and went again, but was always reluctant to leave London. Then, after a few false starts, she finally stayed.

I worried about how it would be with her and Alyssia. It was a long time since Nan had had a toddler around her. But it was all right. They took to each other and Alyssia would run into her room in the morning and jump on her bed.

'Morning, Nanny! Morning, Nanny!'

And then we'd go for walks together and it took her mind off things back in London. I think having Alyssia around ultimately made the transition easier and the bond between my daughter and my grandmother grew as the days passed into weeks and months. Alyssia and I loved to sing together to the radio and Nan found this light-heartedness a little alien at first. But she eventually came round to our way of acting and started joining in, and the three of us were like the Sugababes in the kitchen, singing and dancing together. It was a happy time for me – probably the happiest I'd ever been in my life.

Nan was always a very active person and Birmingham was somewhere new for her to explore. She'd go down to the local shops and come back an hour later, after talking to everyone on the way there and back. My life changed again when she moved in with me. I started to put on weight and we went out exploring together every day and I dressed like a woman again, not like a man. I got myself a PC and started buying and selling stuff online, which gave me a job I could do and still take care of Alyssia the way I wanted to. I wasn't introverted any more and was beginning to become a normal person.

Just like everyone else.

One day I decided it would be a good time to talk about the cancer. I told Nan what had happened, without giving her all the gory details, but the panic alarm inside her went off and I couldn't stop her calling my father. Within a matter of hours, the whole family was in the maisonette in Thirlmere Drive. Alyssia ran and hid behind the sofa because she'd never seen so many big people in such a small space. My father was very concerned.

'Why didn't you tell us, Shelley?'

'It's all right, Dad. It's gone.'

'How d'you know?'

'The doctors told me.'

He wanted to go round the hospital to find out for himself, but I showed him the notes and letters and it settled him down a bit. My uncle John was next.

'You gotta take it easy, Shelley. Don't eat sugar. Stop smoking. Drink green tea.'

Then my uncle Daniel.

'If you need anything, I'm always here for you, Shelley. If anything happens, me and Diane will take care of Alyssia, don't worry.'

That upset Dad.

'What's gonna happen? She said it's gone!'

'I just meant —'

'Don't say things like that, Dan!'

There was nearly a fight. Nan had to intervene and tell them all to leave, because they were stressing me and that wasn't good. The original plan had been for her to stay in Birmingham just until things straightened themselves out in London, but now she decided to stay – permanently.

'I'm going nowhere!'

She told them this so they could all stop worrying. She'd be here to take care of me and Alyssia. Then she shooed them all out and made a pot of tea.

And so we lived together at Thirlmere Drive – me, Nan and Alyssia, for the next four years. I considered going back to work, just part-time. But Nan was nervous about being left on her own. She was seventy-five when she moved in with me and I couldn't leave her in charge of a full-of-energy four-year-old. It wouldn't have been fair on either of them. I thought about bar work in the evenings, but I hated pubs and I believed it would cause more problems than it would cure. I was originally inspired to paint wall murals when I visited prisons as a child and I would have liked to start my own art business. But I'd have had to go into people's houses to measure up and plan – and Nan would have had to come with me. That would've been like taking a tomcat into a pigeon loft. Feathers would have flown. So, instead, we lived closely and were happy and the bonds between us grew. Three women together and we didn't need any man in our lives to complicate things. It was a quiet time – a time of stability and sunshine. We relied on each other for strength and motivation. Nan needed me and I needed Nan. Alyssia needed me and I needed Alyssia. We lived and sang and danced our way through the days and kept the anxiety of the world at bay.

But it couldn't last, could it? Nan always spoke her mind and she could be quite abrasive when she disagreed with something or someone. She had to fight her corner and would never back down from anything. Her familiarity with the locals in the area eventually bred contempt. She'd come back from the shops and say she'd had a row with someone. Then another. And another. It was all right in southeast London where she was well known as the matriarch of the Mackenney clan, but it was different up here and things soon got difficult. It started with the women, but soon their husbands and sons got involved and there were threats and intimidation.

'Why don't you lot bugger off back down south?'

'Don't come up here telling us what to think!'

'If you want it, you can have it!'

I was worried about Alyssia. What if something started on the street and she got caught up in the middle of it? I wanted to tell the police, but Nan wouldn't have any of that.

'It's because of the police I'm up 'ere in the first place, Shell.'

I had to resist the urge to pack up and run again, back to a safe house – a refuge. It took all my energy and will-power to resist the instinct, but I didn't want to put Alyssia through that.

I thought of leaving with Nan, of going back to London with her and taking Alyssia with us. But although I wanted to get away from Thirlmere Drive, I wasn't at all convinced that London was the best option. It held nothing but bad memories for me and there would be nowhere to hide this time. No way out if things went wrong again. Nan suggested we go for a visit first – just to see if it would work. Two weeks to test the water. We wouldn't have to go to 49 Crutchley Road as my father had moved back into the old house round the corner, where my mother deserted me. We could stay there.

'Everything's been sorted, Shell. You don't need to be afraid.'

But I was. I was afraid the old me would be there, waiting. Shaking. Stressing.

My father came up and collected us. Alyssia and me got in the back and Nan sat up front with him. They were happy that I'd agreed to come back, if only for two weeks, and Alyssia was all excited to be going somewhere new.

But I was in turmoil. My stomach was turning over and I felt sick.

The anxiety got worse when we entered London. I was watching through the window as familiar streets passed by. Little seeds of memory began to sprout. My father kept pointing to places.

'Hey, Shelley, do you remember the time . . .'

I didn't. But it was easier to say yes. This was going against all my instincts. My mind was screaming at me to turn round and go back. But I couldn't. By the time we pulled into Crutchley Road, I was practically paranoid. Nan's house was in a cul-de-sac around the corner and I couldn't see it, which was just as well. I knew I couldn't have gone in there. We stopped outside the old house, the one that represented so much sadness, despair and worthlessness, and those feelings came rushing back, almost overpowering me. It took a moment or two for my legs to stop shaking when I got out of the car. It didn't feel like coming home, it felt alien – like I'd been away for a million years and my memory had disintegrated into a mass of squirming maggots. It wasn't me walking up the path to the front door – or rather, it *was* me, but I was in someone else's body.

The house was just as I remembered it. Everything seemed untouched since the last time I'd been there. But I felt like an intruder – a ghost, haunting the place. I put my suitcase away and settled Alyssia in and Nan made a pot of tea. Then we all went to a pie and mash café. I'd always loved London pie and mash and I'd missed it in Birmingham. We drove past the shops I used to go to on my way to school, the bus stop for Catford shopping, the fish shop for takeaways. They were where they'd always been, where they belonged. It was me who didn't belong there. I was getting cramps in my stomach and my appetite disappeared – even for pie and mash. I pushed the food around on my plate until Dad drove us home.

Two days into being back, I had sickness and diarrhoea. Nan decided some fresh air would do me good and she insisted we walk to the local shops. On the way, we passed people and they kept looking at me and saying things to me.

'How are you, Shelley?'

'You're looking well, Shelley.'

'Haven't seen you in ages, Shelley.'

'You all right, Shelley?'

I didn't recognize any of them. We stopped to speak to a woman about my age. Nan chatted to her for a minute or so, then we moved on.

'Who was that, Nan?'

'Don't you know?'

'No.'

'Your cousin, Rachel.'

I had to walk slightly behind Nan because I couldn't remember the route. It was a walk I'd taken thousands of times, but it was like I'd never been there before. I was glad to get back to the house.

The first week filtered by and I managed to get through it. But then Nan wanted to go to Catford High Street. We drove there with Dad and here, strangely, I could remember everything: shops I'd bought stuff in, stores I'd browsed, restaurants I'd eaten in. I was acutely aware of people around me, crowding me, crushing me. Did they know me? Did I know them? I couldn't breathe. The florists that sent Nan the flowers, the shop where I bought my magazines, the supermarket for food, clothes, CDs, DVDs, cookers, shopping addiction. The bank! Everything started to whirl round. Flashbacks. Memories. Images everywhere. I felt like a freak. On display – everybody laughing and pointing. I had to get out of there. Panic. Heart thumping, thumping, thumping.

My father saw the terror in my face and he took us away before I collapsed. I knew then I didn't want to be in London. Couldn't be in London. There were too many reminders of who I was. What I was.

We went back to Birmingham before the end of the second week.

20

Writing

When I moved into Thirlmere Drive, I was in heaven. I loved the place. It was a little piece of paradise. I'd been happy there for a long time, but now it had turned sour and it was getting more intolerable by the day, more preju- diced and partisan. I needed to move again – to run away. But this time I had to take Nan and Alyssia with me. The council said they couldn't give me another place as I was too far down the list. But the local animosity towards us was growing, getting worse. Nan couldn't go outside the maisonette without getting into a fight. She was pushing on for eighty, but she could still have a scrap with women a third of her age. It became a 'them and us' situation, with a lot more of them than us. And I couldn't stop Nan having a go at them – it was just her nature. I also didn't want my father and uncles getting involved, because then it would have become an all-out war. I was constantly try- ing to diffuse the situation and it was pulling me to pieces.

People might say it was Nan's fault, but it wasn't – not all of it. Nan was just Nan and would never change and I loved her. She'd done so much for me and been a mother to me when I had none. I'd left her and caused her pain, when I owed her so much. Now we were together again and I wasn't going to allow these people to pull us apart. So I took her side and we were the Mackenneys against the world again. But it was taking its toll on me, both physically and mentally.

The depression started to come back and my doctor put me on antidepressants and sleeping tablets. But they didn't suit me, they just turned me into a zombie. The crunch came with a big argument in the middle of the street, when Alyssia was really upset. I decided I couldn't put up with it any longer. I went to the council and told them that Thirlmere Drive was now a health hazard for myself and my daughter. I said my grandmother had come to live with me for protection and we were overcrowded. I told them if I had to keep living there my depression would get worse and my mental health would be jeopardized. They let me fill out a re-housing application, but they didn't hold out much hope.

So I went on the offensive.

I got supporting letters from my doctor and from Alyssia's school and from Women's Aid and from Age UK on behalf of Nan. I contacted my MP and anyone else who might be able to help and I provided a list of the medication I was on. I gave them access to my medical history and a supporting letter from the hospital where I was treated for cancer. It took nine months of trying to move heaven and earth, but they finally transferred us to a three-bedroom house, away from Thirlmere Drive.

In August 2010, I moved to the place where I still live today.

The three of us settled into our new home, and peace and stability returned. It was better here, as it wasn't such a tight little community like Thirlmere Drive had been. People were more anonymous and liked to mind their own business – and that suited me down to the ground. Nan kept her distance from the neighbours and things worked out very well.

Nan had been going on for some time about how she'd always wanted to write a book about my grandfather 'Big H' Mackenney – how he was framed for five murders and spent twenty years in prison for crimes he didn't commit, before being released on appeal and getting the conviction quashed. I believed this was something I could help her do from home and still be there to look after Alyssia when she came in from school. The trouble was, I didn't have a clue about the book business or how to go about getting it published. But, like everything else I'd done, I set about finding out.

I read some true-life crime books to get an idea of what people wanted and I made a list of publishers and authors who were writing those sorts of memoirs and biographies. It was difficult getting contact details for the authors, so I wrote up a good sales letter, setting out what I thought the merits of the book were and its possibilities and potential markets. I was a top seller at the bank, so I was good at sales pitching. I sent the letter to the authors of some crime books, via their publishers, and we got some positive responses – but they all eventually petered out and came to nothing. They said there wasn't a big enough market for such a book and, because of her age, they doubted if Nan would be able to write it. We contacted author after author but, for one reason or another, none of them were interested in getting involved.

A year passed without any success and I decided to try

a different approach. I wrote directly to the publishers with just the seed of the story, hoping to entice them. Most of them didn't even reply and those who did said the true-crime genre was old and played out. But I knew Nan had an extraordinary tale to tell and I was determined not to give up. One publisher finally asked for a synopsis, but I didn't know what this was or how to write it. I decided we needed some help. I searched the Internet and found a professional ghostwriter, who took the project on, wrote up a formal book proposal and introduced us to a literary agent, who then pitched the book proposal to publishers. That was how it was done professionally. Now I knew! Finally, we were getting somewhere. A publisher came back and said they weren't interested in Big H's story, but they would be interested in a book about Nan's life. She'd had so many remarkable experiences, going back to the slums of London in the 1930s, through the war years and being evacuated as a child, into the post-war years and the gangs of south London, then into the 1960s and 1970s as the matriarch of a notorious family whose husband was in prison for murder after a very public show trial.

In the meantime, everyone was telling us we were crazy, that we'd never get a book published. They thought we were getting a bit above our station in even trying. They laughed when Nan said she was going to write her memoirs, but this only made me more determined to succeed.

We had to go down to London to meet the literary agent and the publisher for Nan to sign contracts and all that stuff. The day before we were due to travel, Nan got very ill with a stomach bug and she was vomiting during the night. I thought we wouldn't make it and the whole thing would go up in smoke. But Nan was a tough soldier. She forced herself out of bed and we went down and she did the business. Nan was such a colourful character and in the meeting with the publisher she had them all enthralled with the stories of her hard life. I could see they were amazed. They'd never met anyone like Eileen Mackenney before – and probably wouldn't ever again.

So, Nan signed the contracts and was given a deadline to deliver the book. Now all she had to do was write it. The way we worked it was, Nan would talk and I'd write it all down and then send the material to the ghost. He'd send me back queries and questions and I'd get the answers from Nan. I was the go-between, the intermediary. But I was learning about the process of writing, about producing a book. And it wasn't as easy as I first thought it would be. I'm sure there are many people who've thought about writing a book, but don't really appreciate the amount of work involved. I know I didn't. Nan was taken ill again in the middle of the writing with a severe chest infection. We'd been working on the book every day to meet the deadline and I was worried we'd fall behind. The doctor put her on a course of steroids that gave her loads of energy and she ended up waking me at 3.00 a.m. every morning and we'd sit there in our pyjamas with a pot of tea. She'd talk and I'd write for hours and hours. I'd keep going till my eyes hurt and my fingers seized up.

At last it was done and it went away to the publisher for editing and proofing, and we waited. *Borstal Girl* finally came out in 2011 and it was a bestseller. All the people who laughed at us in the beginning weren't laughing any more. I felt so proud! It was such an achievement.

Suddenly, all the work was worth it – all the early mornings and late nights – and it had given me a real purpose in life. The missing girl who'd been sleeping on the streets just a few years previously had helped make a dream come true. The aftermath was radio and magazine and newspaper interviews for Nan. I went with her and she was in her element, because she always liked to talk and everyone found her amazing and extraordinary. Which I'd always known, of course. Every time she went out in the street she was stopped by strangers who wanted to shake her hand and she loved every minute of it. I built a website and a fan page for her and I got involved in promoting the book. It was a world I adapted to easily and felt at home in. I'm still contacted daily by my grandmother's fans who ask when the book will be made into a film or a television series and I know that several producers are interested in doing just that.

So watch this space!

One day, when I was out shopping with Nan, we passed someone selling *The Big Issue*. Nan turned round and went back and bought a copy. I'd never seen her do that before and she said she just felt sorry for the guy and didn't even want the magazine. I knew it was sold to help homeless people so I thought it was an appropriate gesture and, next day, I started to read it. As I skimmed through, I came across an advertisement that took up half a page.

Do you know anyone who has ever been missing?
Have you ever been missing?
Have you ever walked out of your life for a week?
A month? Maybe longer?

An independent television company was looking for people who'd been reported missing for a documentary they were making, and there was a contact telephone number. I showed it to Nan.

'Shell, that's you. You should ring them.'

I'd never spoken about my life as a missing person to anyone – not even my own family. It was a time when I'd fallen to pieces and had to rebuild myself. No, I couldn't tell anyone else about it. It was a private thing that I kept inside me, locked away from prying eyes.

I put the magazine to one side, but I kept thinking about the advert. If I could help Nan write her bestseller, maybe I could do this. Maybe people needed to know what it was like to go missing, physically and emotionally; why people went missing; what it took to just up and walk out of your life; what made someone do something as desperate as that. I knew the answers. I'd done it. Should I call them? I decided I would, just to find out what was involved. It wouldn't hurt to check it out – see what they wanted – but I'd approach with caution. In all my time being gone, I'd never met another missing person – oh, I'd met many girls who'd left home because of abuse, but never anyone who was actually 'missing', like me. So I was curious to see what kind of response they got to the advert, if there were lots of people contacting them and, if so, whether they'd found a corresponding cause – a common denominator.

The producers told me the documentary had been commissioned to explore the phenomenon of missing persons from the point of view of the person who went missing and also those left behind. They said they'd spoken to many families who'd had people go missing, but they were having difficulty finding anyone who'd actually gone missing. In fact, up to that point, they hadn't found a single 'missing' person. Except me. They asked if they could come visit me and I agreed. The meeting was very informal, but Nan got upset when I started talking about my breakdown. So one of them went with her into the front room to keep her calm, while I continued in the kitchen.

I gave them a condensed version of what happened: the pressure – running – the refuge – being homeless – finding myself again – finding my family again. They were quite excited about it and asked if they could include me in the documentary, as they hadn't found anyone else who'd gone missing and come in out of the cold again. They said they wanted to give hope to families that some people do come back, no matter how long they've been gone. And also to the missing themselves. There could be people out there who were afraid to come back, afraid to face what they'd run away from. I liked their raison d'être, as I could totally relate to it. And maybe my story might help someone make a decision to pick up that phone and make a call. So I agreed to do it. It felt like it was meant to be, what with Nan going back to buy the magazine, me finding the advert and making the call. Maybe it was something I was meant to do.

If what happened to me could actually help other people, then maybe I could turn my experience into something positive: help others, reach out to them, show them how to face their fears and let them see that they could come back and change things. Maybe they'd see me in the documentary and understand there was someone else out there who understood their isolation and loneliness. If it came good for me, then maybe it could come good for them too. If it could help even one person, then it had to be worth doing. When you run, you become someone else. Anonymous. You start again and forget the past. It's so easy to keep moving and not look back at the devastation you've left behind. But the euphoria of breaking free eventually wears off or stays as a facade – a shell – and you think, 'I can't go back now. I've done too much, hurt too many, gone too far.' But you can. You can always reconnect.

Arm's length.

Filming the documentary was done in a private house in King's Heath. It took three or four hours and I talked and talked and talked.

Then, my ghostwriter contacted me and asked if I'd be interested in writing my own memoir, as a kind of follow-up to Nan's. I probably wouldn't have agreed if I hadn't already done the documentary. I didn't think a book would be any different. I was wrong! The book was much more difficult. Talking on camera is one thing, but a book puts every tiny detail under the microscope. There's nowhere to hide. You're totally exposed. The ghost asked all the hard questions and expected honest answers. He haunted me! Unless you're a celebrity, people aren't going to buy your memoir to find out what you like for lunch or what your favourite colour is. They want to know about the things that make you tick, the tiny intimate things. They want to get under your skin – inside your head. It hurt!

I thought doing my own book would be easier than Nan's, where I had to sit typing for hours while Nan talked. This was my story and I could tell it in my own words and at my own pace. I soon found myself on a roller-coaster of emotion, as I was brought back down into deep memory, really having to remember the things that caused my nervous breakdown. Reliving them. Reaching down into the detail and dissecting my psyche to under-stand and explain. It made me think all over again about my actions, about my flaws and my faults, my weaknesses, my shortcomings. It brought me back down to my most basic level, to my lowest point, and I went to bed some nights feeling totally depressed and reliving the feelings of desperation I'd had back then. Putting my life into words was incredibly hard. I was deconstructing myself all over again and, years after the events, after the counsel-ling, after coming back, this book taught me that I was still learning about myself.

But after the deconstruction came the reconstruction and I remembered my strengths, the changes in me, the things I'd learned along the way. The woman I was now. Writing the book was therapeutic in a way nothing else has ever been. I can understand my actions now in a way I couldn't before. But, even up to the end, I found myself questioning whether I was doing the right thing or not. I'd made a lot of mistakes and I was ashamed of many things I'd done and I deeply regretted the pain I'd caused to people. It was difficult enough to admit these things to myself, let alone put them in a book for the whole world to read. But I believed it was a story that needed to be told and, in telling it, maybe I could make people more aware of the missing, the forgotten, the wanderers, the misfits, the lost and the vulnerable.

Maybe the next time you see them on the street you'll realize they are real people and give them a second thought.

I would never recommend what I did to anyone else. The situations I've been in and the things I've been through could have been fatal. It was sheer luck that I walked away from it all unscathed. There are many opportunists out there, waiting like vultures to pounce on the innocent and naive, the weak and vulnerable. I've seen it over and over again. A typical scenario is that a girl feels left out at home because her mum's got a new boyfriend. The boyfriend tries it on with the girl and the mum blames the girl and chucks her out. The girl is alone and feeling rejected. She walks down the street and meets someone full of charm who listens to her and flatters her and offers to help her. He buys her drink and offers her drugs. He gives her all the attention that she was missing at home, someone to talk to, someone who understands. He draws her in. It's a gradual thing until the girl trusts him implicitly and loves him unconditionally. Then it changes. The girl is made to become an object to earn him money or to satisfy his friends. Or both. And she does it. Because she depends on him.

Running away opened my eyes to many things. I was blind to what goes on before then. I met girls and heard stories of torment and abuse so bad that I wished I hadn't been told them in the first place. I wished I could remove them from my head. And I realized my problems, my breakdown, paled into insignificance compared to the horror stories I was hearing. I felt ashamed at my selfishness – ashamed at the endless hours I spent feeling sorry for myself, when I was looking at girls who'd suffered unimaginable hurt and torture, and they were sitting close to me, smiling and laughing. I couldn't understand how they could find it in themselves to laugh, to want to carry on living at all.

And if this book is read by someone like that – someone on the run from some horror – maybe they'll take a crumb of comfort in their darkness and depression. I wanted death to come to me once; I welcomed it as a friend, as a relief from the unending torment of my life. I was on the edge and looking down into the abyss. But I came back from it and I'm glad I did. I learned how to live again – earned the right to live again. I rediscovered the joy in simple things and in knowing that I didn't need a lot to be at peace with myself. If I'd died when I wanted to, all those years ago, I'd never have experienced the love I feel now, the love I have now, the love I give and receive back in return.

Finally, I need to say 'sorry' to the people I walked away from. I can only imagine how they must have felt, especially in the beginning, when they had no idea where I was or what had happened to me. And I've never forgotten the acts of kindness people showed me during my days of chaos and confusion.

I'm so sorry.

Thank you.

And thank *you*.

For reading my book.

I hope it helps.

Epilogue

Sometimes life is like breaking a person down to their most basic level and putting them back together again. What comes back isn't what went in. Bits are missing or added or changed about. The same ingredients, but a different person. To this day I have problems crying and feelings can sometimes get locked away and compacted. Outwardly, I can appear unaffected – indifferent – cold, even. But underneath it's another story. Emotionally, I'm very restrained. I don't let my feelings out easily. I won't fight or argue with people, I just walk away and don't express anything, and this can infuriate them, even though it's not meant to. It's just the way I am – the way I was made. Or became. And even though I'm older and wiser now, the little girl is still somewhere inside and she can be heard crying at times when things are silent and strained.

But I still love to sing – and dance. I do both with Alyssia and it's great. She's getting older and we're good together. I can't play some of the music I used to listen to, it brings back all the sadness and how close I came to giving up. But the harmonies in my heart kept me going through the bad times and they're still there.

I have polycystic ovary syndrome to this day, which knocks my hormones off balance and causes infertility and mood swings, and the bleeding comes and goes when it wants to. But, as long as it's not cancer, I'm not worried. I'm now smear tested every year and, in 2012, the test came back with abnormalities and I had to have a colposcopy again. They wanted to take a biopsy, but my cervix is so damaged the scar tissue is too thick for a biopsy. In the end, they decided that the abnormalities were caused by the scar tissue and nothing else needed to be done. So far so good! It also means I'll never be able to carry another child. I have hardly any cervix left, so Alyssia is the only experience of being a mother I'll ever have. That's one of the reasons she's so precious to me.

If anyone was to ask for my advice about the downside of life, I'd tell them to talk. Talk. Always talk about what's going on inside you. Don't keep it to yourself. I know it's hard and sometimes more difficult to talk to people you know than to a stranger. But you're never alone, like I thought I was. Letting feelings out lets the darkness out with them and being able to open up lets in the light. When you're down and depressed, it's easy to imagine everyone's against you and judging you, everyone thinks you're going crazy. There's nothing good any more. Nothing positive. But, believe me, if you ask for help you'll find it. And it's not a weakness, it's a strength. It's recognizing a problem and not ignoring it. After all, truth is never absolute, it's multiple and contradictory and always a matter of interpretation. Only knowledge can recognize truth – real truth. And truth creates more knowledge.

I wanted to go back into education, to finish what I should have done all that time ago. I even went to a college careers advisor who told me I could do an access course and then a degree at university – either biomedical science or something in business. But I decided against it in the end because Nan was getting older and more frail and didn't like being left on her own. I'm not ruling it out for the future, although a formal education is one thing and the school of life is entirely another. I learned a lot when I went missing – how to appreciate things and be thankful, instead of always feeling empty and disconnected and buying endless bits of junk to fill the emotional gap in my heart. Now I can look around and see all the good and wonderful things that cost nothing and I'm content. I've learned that, no matter how bad things are, there's always someone worse off – having it harder and tougher – suffering their own personal misery.

I was once in my own selfish little space, like some people today who think the whole world was put there for their convenience. Everything they hear is the static of want. They want this and they want that. Want, want, want – all the time is spent wanting, listening to the want static. But desire can destroy. Now I understand what it feels like to have nothing, to be down and out, to feel lost and lonely, and my priorities have changed. Now I've learned to take only what's needed, not what's wanted. I've learned to identify need. And it takes discipline to control desire – to distinguish it from need.

I've learned how to forgive myself too, to stop beating myself up for past mistakes. I had some ideal in my head about what I had to become, but now I realize I don't *have* to become anything. In exploring the small physical world around me, I've explored the large metaphysical world inside me and I think I know myself now. Maybe not completely, I don't think that will ever happen, but enough to like myself. And it's something I never thought I'd be able to do. A lot of the issues I had when I was younger never left me completely, but I've learned to live with them. I know how they affect me and how I can cope with them. And even now I haven't completely outgrown the undiagnosed disassociation disorder. I can still shut down and forget things that hurt me. While writing this book, I had to really struggle to remember what happened because my natural instinct was to block it all out, to bury it. But it's OK, I'm learning to cope with it. I understand now that life is a work in progress. Things happen every day: feelings surface, problems occur, mistakes are made. But they can be turned round and made positive by pragmatism.

Of course, there are always exceptions to every rule. I've been back to London many times. I realized not everything there was bad and some things left good memories in my mind. But I've still never been back to Nan's house at 49 Crutchley Road. I can't even go look at the house. Every time I try, my legs shake and I'm filled with the same sadness I had back then, when I lived there. So, I suppose some things will never change.

I used to have lots of plans and ambitions when I was at the bank but, because they all fell apart, I'm very careful not to set myself up for that kind of disappointment again. But I would like to believe that I can achieve something in life. I'd like to be independent and to show Alyssia a different way. I'd like her to know she can achieve her dreams if she works hard enough for them. I'd like to be proud of her and I'd like her to be proud of me. I honestly don't know what the future holds – and I don't mean that in a negative way. I really have no idea which path my life will follow through the months and years, or where that path will take me. So many possibilities present themselves when you're open and accepting – when you're willing to explore life in all its guises and get-ups. And if that path crosses the paths of others who are troubled, I'd like to be able to pass on my experiences and the lessons I've learned in a positive way that's not preachy or patronizing. To say that happiness is there – for those who know where to find it.

Everything I've been through in my life has changed me. And I'm still changing, evolving into the person I'll be when I die. I haven't met that woman yet and I hope it'll be a long time until I do. But I'm no longer a facade. I'm real. Words like 'rejection' and 'failure' don't have the same resonance as they once did. And what do they mean anyway? They're just the interpretations of other people. And I'm not ashamed of who I am. I'm not looking for a place to fit in – the place I'm in fits me. I made that place myself and it suits me. Everything I needed to find was inside me all the time and I'm still discovering – still finding things.

When Alyssia gets older and makes a life for herself, I hope we'll still be as close as we are now. If she ever feels lost or confused, she can come back to me – and if I'm not there, then maybe reading this book will reassure her that things are not so terrible and there's nothing that can't be overcome by love and time. Maybe she'll lie in the dead of night and look up at the stars, just like I used to do on that narrow ledge on the roof of the flat in Noel

Road. No noise – no mayhem – no tumult. Just endless space peppered with pinholes of light, sparkling specks of eternity. She might lie there and absorb the wonder of it all – the endless ceaselessness of existence.

And she'll know –

I'm looking back at her.

PENGUIN BOOKS

Missing

Shelley Mackenney lives in Birmingham with her grandmother Eileen, the author of *Borstal Girl*, and her beloved daughter Alyssia.